A Modern Priest Looks At His Outdated Church has been called "the most challenging and controversial" spiritual book of our times. Written by a young Catholic priest, Fr. James Kavanaugh, it rocked the religious world as few books in history have. This book replaced medieval myths about sin and hell, with the courage of private conscience and personal contact with a loving God. With a new introduction and conclusion by its author, *A Modern Priest* enlightens another generation struggling with the same basic issues.

"Here is what millions have felt and what desperately needed to be said. This book will move the world."
—Psychology Today

"There is no question that the churches as well as the synagogues are in many ways outdated.... Religion, like science, goes through a process of evolution...Kavanaugh has done much to further this revolution
—Issac Bashevis Singer

"Brilliantly worded, thoroughly readable...bears on several counts a striking resemblance to Martin Luther."
—San Francisco Chronicle

"...A personal cry of anguish that goes right to the heart of the troubles currently plaguing the Roman Catholic Church."
—The New York Times Book Review

"Few will doubt the realism of this narrative."
—Christopher Kauffman

"...It is strong medicine from a brave and honest priest."
—Justus George Lawler

A MODERN PRIEST LOOKS AT HIS OUTDATED CHURCH

25th Anniversary Edition

A MODERN PRIEST LOOKS AT HIS OUTDATED CHURCH

By Father James Kavanaugh

 Steven J. Nash Publishing
P. O. Box 2115
Highland Park, Illinois 60035

A Modern Priest Looks At His Outdated Church

Hardback edition first published by Trident Press, a division of Simon and Schuster. Paperback edition first published by Pocket Books, a division of Simon and Schuster. Printed in the United States of America.

Library of Congress Catalogue #92-080924
    Kavanaugh, James J.
     A Modern Priest Looks At His Outdated Church

     ISBN # 1-878995-16-2   First Steven J. Nash Publihing Edition
                                   Copyright © 1992 by James Kavanaugh

---

To all who have loved me
just the way I am

YOU ARE YOUR OWN ANSWER

You are your own answer,
Beyond books and seers, psychics or doctors
Beyond the strength that comes
from what you have accomplished.
Your weakness is as valuable as your strength,
Your helplessness as loveable as your charm.
You are God's child and each step of the way,
He gives you bread and not a stone,
food and not a serpent.
All is part of the plan, as you look within
And listen to the quiet, persistent voice
that tells you who you are....

From *Quiet Water*

BOOKS BY JAMES KAVANAUGH

NON-FICTION

There's Two Of You
Man In Search of God
Journal of Renewal
A Modern Priest Looks At His Outdated Church
The Struggle of the Unbeliever (Limited Edition)
The Birth of God
Between Man And Woman(co-authored)
Search: A Guide For Those Who Dare

POETRY

There Are Men Too Gentle To Live Among Wolves
Will You Be My Friend?
America: A Ballad
The Crooked Angel (a children's book)
Sunshine Days And Foggy Nights
Maybe If I Loved You More
Winter Has Lasted Too Long
Walk Easy On The Earth
Laughing Down Lonely Canyons
Today I Wondered About Love
(Adapted from: Faces In The City)
From Loneliness To Love
Tears and Laughter Of A Man's Soul
Mystic Fire: The Love Poetry Of James Kavanaugh
Quiet Water: The Inspirational Poetry of James Kavanaugh

FICTION

A Coward For Them All
The Celibates

ALLEGORY

Celebrate The Sun: A Love Story
A Village Called Harmony—A Fable

25 YEARS LATER

Twenty five years ago I wrote *A Modern Priest Looks At His Outdated Church*. It was not a book I had intended to write. I had taken leave from my priesthood because I knew that my Church was not a reflection of what Jesus had taught. I watched our bishops return from the II Vatican Council and saw them still too untrusting and terrified to make changes of real substance. Latin was changed to English, Gregorian chant gave way to hymns, and the altar faced the people.

But the control of human minds remained unchanged. The secret screams of spiritually battered men and women were not addressed! My Church still was invading bedrooms, abusing consciences, distorting sex, manufacturing sin, patronizing other sects, dishonoring women, turning custom to law and loving myths to angry dogmas. Sincere souls were condemned or threatened with a hell that never was. But most of all, it continued to discredit the voice of God that speaks to each of us in private revelation.

It was that voice within me that impelled me to write. It was not a choice, but an inner, irresistible force that empowered and at times dictated what I wrote. The words flowed passionately, almost effortlessly, and I felt more like a spectator than an author. The impact of those words was beyond anything I could imagine. I had no idea the book would reach millions of people in seven different languages, that it would lead thousands of priests and nuns from the Church, drive the pope himself to preach from the Vatican balcony, and give support to countless people of every religion to follow their own inner light. I only wrote because I had to, but it became clear that my struggle was like their own.

Their letters told me that, like myself, they hungered for a God of love and compassion, not the familiar control of a frightened parent that restricts our vision and pillages our dignity. We could no longer endure such a God. Thus we did not leave the Church, we outgrew it! We wanted more than it offered. If we were to be spiritual adults, we had to put away the things of a child. Custom and comfort were not of consequence if they did not lead to the joy and freedom of God's own Son. Later I wrote of "My Easy God" Who only asked blind adherence to institutional precepts and sanctions:

> I have lost my easy God—the one whose name
>   I knew since childhood
> I knew his temper, his sullen outrage, his ritual forgiveness...
>   I never told him how he frightened me,
>   how he followed me as a child
> When I played with friends or begged for candy
>   on Halloween...
> He the mysterious took all mystery away,
>   corroded my imagination,
> Controlled the stars and would not let them
>   speak for themselves.
> Now he haunts me seldom: some fierce umbilical is broken.
> I live with my own fragile hopes and sudden rising despair.
>   Now I do not weep for my sins; I have
>   learned to love them and
> To know that they are the wounds that make love real...
> I walk alone, but not so terrified as when he held my hand...
>   Perhaps I have no God—what does it matter?
> I have beauty and joy and transcending loneliness,
> I have the beginning of love—as beautiful as it is feeble,
>   As free as it is human...
> I sense the call of creation, I feel its swelling in my hands,
>   I can lust and love, eat and drink, sleep and rise,
> But my easy God is gone—and in his stead
>   The mystery of loneliness and love.

From *There Are Men Too Gentle To Live Among Wolves*

Hundreds of talk shows and interviews, lectures and debates, convinced me I had to surrender my "easy God" to find the God within. While speaking at Notre Dame University, that inner voice compelled me to put aside my prepared text and publicly resign my priesthood. Again it was not a choice but an unexpected demand! As I studied the intense faces, I could no longer defend the indefensible or teach what I did not believe to emerging groups of sincere and spiritually starved young people. The Church had defined God in an effort to control Him, and despite superficial reforms, it still ignored the inner voice of God within each of us—from Rome to Bombay, from Mecca and Jerusalem to Chicago.

For a time I continued to fight the Church, determined to reform it. It gradually became clear that what I asked of the Church, I must find myself. The Church was not yet ready or able to change, so without a blueprint, I began my own search for the God I had lost in earliest childhood. My path has been slow and arduous because I've had to release most of what I spent my life learning and teaching. Fear and guilt run deep and I had been trained in it by experts. Thus I had few inner skills for such a journey. I was as controlled and controlling, as judgmental and frightened as my Church had ever been.

It was Hippocrates who said that pain is a cruel doctor but few of us learn from any other. What all the Holy Weeks and gospel narratives, the crucifixes and sermons, the prayers and theology had never taught me, life did. I had lost my Catholic community and lifelong friends, my marriage failed, publishers turned away, three older brothers died of cancer in their prime, and I felt the ravages of buried fear and depression. I was not really prepared for the simple message of death and resurrection that is the core of every religion: "Unless the grain of wheat falls into the ground and dies, it remains itself alone." Like the Jews in exodus from Egypt or Jesus in his desert, it appears that we must confront each illusion that promises peace, then denies it. So must the Church.

I still feel a connection with the Church that has been an integral part of my culture and journey to God. My fervent wish is that both of us will continue to grow in the wisdom and understanding, the compassion and love that only death and resurrection can teach. Jesus said it all, but somehow his message got lost among the historic refuse of creeds and commandments, sin and judgment, fear, guilt and eternal torments. We only have to learn not to rule but to serve, not to judge and condemn, but to honor everyone of any cult or culture as God's own offspring. We have to die to live. So does the Church.

I decided to reissue *Modern Priest* not only to honor numerous requests, but because I realize how much of it remains relevant 25 years later. The Church is still afraid to trust men and women, to let go of the past, to scrape history's scars from the power and beauty of the message of Jesus. Like the rest of us, it still has a lot of "dying" to do before it rises.

There is so much help and understanding needed in our world. Such great hunger for spiritual guidance! For love and laughter, compassion and service, generosity and peace! The same history that made us separate and afraid can make us whole! A generation has passed since I wrote, and yet the institutional Church has not evolved with the spiritual consciousness of an ever shrinking world. It is my hope that even twenty five years later, *A Modern Priest Looks At His Outdated Church* can continue to play a part in that transformation. Writing it was a directive from my inner voice and the beginning of a journey that has brought me closer to God, to myself, and to you. I hope that reading it may do the same for another.

PREFACE AND DEDICATION

When I wrote the article "I Am a Priest, I Want to Marry" for *The Saturday Evening Post*,[1] I had no intention of writing a book. I had not the time or the need. When the letters came in response to my article, however, I knew that I must start again. The letters came in bundles, hundreds of them, from many continents, and I read each word with the hunger of a man who truly wanted to learn. There were as many from Protestants as from Catholics.[2] Children wrote, nuns and priests wrote, the feeble and tired hands of the aged wrote. It was a procession of warm hearts that passed before my eyes and opened to me as I had opened to them. Most of all, the wounded wrote. The story of my soul had opened the scars in their own. The letters were more eloquent than anything I could describe, since they were written in innocent blood. They told me of pains that far surpassed mine, and they begged me to speak for them so that all the world could hear.

Some of the letters scolded me as a spoiled son who wanted the best of both worlds. Some called me insincere, a "Judas," a "crybaby" who could not live with the promise he had made. Some told me that I had no right to happiness because life had offered them only grief and disillusionment. Some called me a "dangerous minority," a "deluded and lost soul," a "sentimental fool."

Most, however—ten to one, in fact—approved of what I said. One woman moved me to tears when she wrote: "If such as you walk away, who will stay to care for the sheep? Please don't go, stay and fight for justice!" Priests wrote and told me of the senseless struggle, the loves they had known and surrendered. Women wrote who loved priests and had lost them to the righteousness of law. Priests who had left and married wrote and asked that I understand the loneliness of exile from memories and friends. Protestants offered me shelter in their parish, bishops offered me work in their Episcopal diocese. Mormons offered love and family in a life of service in the Church.

Most of all, the suffering wrote, and begged me to write for them. The divorced and lonely, the couples with too many children, those fearful of sex, the spouses of alcoholics and homosexuals, those denied the sacraments, those whose marriage case was never solved, the sinner who could not be absolved—all of them wrote and filled my nights with suffering and shame. I, the unworthy priest, was asked to hear the misery of the Christian world without the power of Christ to make men walk.

I had always loved men as best I could, but now I was asked to love them even more. Names that had never known me told me of their love and concern. Letters poured in from hands that had never responded to an article before. These were not the letters of brief and cold comment, but the personal and touching stories of broken hearts. I had spoken to them and they had answered with the words that no one else had heard.

To these I dedicate my book, to those that have suffered as I, and more. I thank them for trusting me with their wounds, and promise that I will not cease to seek a healing as long as God shall give me breath. I well may lose my priesthood, though its passing would not occur with lack of pain. I shall not lose my faith, though the pressures of my superiors may well reduce it to the faith of a simple man in search of an unknown God. There is one hope that sustains me in the midst of bitter attack: if a thousand men can understand my cry, then God Himself will not dismiss me without mercy. I want to speak for His children, for the lonely and the lost, for the sons who find the faith that satisfied their fathers too narrow to fill their present need. I write not in bitterness, but in love, not in the anger of demolition, but in the challenge of construction.

I need my Church, for without the strength of Christ it gives I cannot live. I have known its comforts for almost forty years, and feel the right to speak out as a son. Can I not be a son, your brother, because I do not think as you, or speak as you? Think before you answer, because I believe my name is legion!

INTRODUCTION

Catholicism as a monolithic structure is disappearing.[1] Once the man who differed with the party line stole quietly away. Now he refuses to abandon his communion with God. From a timid rebellion has grown a courageous confrontation. This is not merely the roar of angry young men. It is the fruit of a tortuous, a studious examination of the foundations of faith. Faith has passed from the passive and complete acceptance of a body of truths to the honest search for total commitment.

The world has become man-centered, meaning-centered, and the individual measures the traditional truths in terms of personal value. He refuses to accept irrelevant sermons, a sterile liturgy, a passé and speculative theology which explores publicly dry and distant formulas, a law which does not explain its own origins. He demands a pastor who reaches him in honest dialogue. He will not be bullied by an authoritarian demand for the observance of parish boundaries, nor by moralizing which ignores the true and complex context of modern life.

The layman has witnessed a more humane eucharistic fast, a more open view of mixed marriages, a more understanding discussion of the birth-control problem and of the dilemma of Catholic education. He has recognized the human face of the Church which has been forced to change its expression or die. This has given him the courage to hope and push for greater changes still.

This book is the account of a priest who has suffered in the leadership of a Church grown arrogant and inhumane. It is the story of a suffering people witnessed in confession and private consultation. It is the story of a suffering Church which often reflects a dishonest theology far more than a divine imperative. This is a book born of the conviction that I can still be a Catholic, that I can still search for God and meaning in a Church which must exchange its authoritarian and regal robe for that of a suffering servant. It is a book which hopes that the world can begin to appreciate our Catholic sincerity and that we, the members, can face a future life of freedom and joy within the Church.

This is not the speculation of a professional theologian, although my education allows me to wear that hat. It is the soul-searching plea of a Christian for an evaluation of what is Christian, and what is simply tired and imperious tradition. I want to be a Christian, but I will not be terrorized into believing that the present structure of the Church is an adequate representation of the Christ of Gospel and history. I merely tell you what Christianity means to me and ask you to reflect and discover if you share a part of my vision. If you do, I want you to struggle with me to bring about its fulfillment. If not, I ask you to tell me why, not to curse me with fleeting words of fear.

I will not give up my faith. Nor will I accept the travesty, born of another age, which caricatures the Christian ideal. Catholicism offers so much that is good and true that its faithful adherents cannot sit by passively and watch it settle into structured idealism. It has so much to say, so much to offer, if only it can recognize the growing and positive drive for personalism in the world. A religion which expects men to march in identical step and to chant a univocal doctrine ceases to draw the atomic man to the holy God.

Vatican II is only a spark, a beginning—but it marks the future with a ray of hope. In the light of its encouragement I would like to describe my vision of the problem of an outdated Church and the direction in which we must move. I do not write for the professional, but for the sincere man, simple or sophisticated, whose living search for meaning moves the professional theologian from his comfortable perch and forces him to examine his presuppositions. I do not ask for a comfortable pew; far from it. I ask for honest dialogue, an open hierarchy, a Church which does not have all the answers or expect all men to walk in the wooden cadence of frozen categories. The recent *Declaration on Religious Freedom* leads me to believe that I do not hope in vain:

The declaration of this Vatican Council on the right of man to religious freedom has its foundation in the dignity of the person, whose exigencies have come to be more fully known to human reason through the centuries of experience. . . . It is one of the major tenets of Catholic doctrine that man's response to God in faith must be free . . . ! [2]

I write to tell the man who has been forced from the faith of his fathers: You can still believe and still be free. You can only believe to the degree that you are free. And so can I.

CONTENTS

A MODERN PRIEST

LOOKS AT HIS

OUTDATED

CHURCH

1. THE IDEAL BECOMES

THE LAW

Once, long ago, in a world of confusion and weariness, there exploded a new and exciting hope. A man appeared in Palestine and spoke in syllables that seemed to come from God. He was a Jew, steeped in the power and beauty of a religious heritage unparalleled in East or West. He was not locked in bigotry nor did he serve the interests of a single nation or a special race. His blood, indeed, was the sensitive and boiling blood of Abraham and David, the blood that would mark the Jewish peoples in ages yet to come. His vision, however, went past the boundaries of Palestine to encompass the world. His eyes looked to everyone who hurt, and his healing hand was extended to the weak and sinful woman, the outcast leper, the blind man who had worn out his friends and relatives with his wailing. Weary men heard him and felt a sudden surge of strength. The guilty listened to him, and began again to respect themselves as men. Fishermen followed him and so did the nobles who had discovered that wine and women did not satisfy each thirsting ache. Some men called him the "God-man," and even those skeptical of his stature marveled at the power of his words.

In a sense he had nothing new to say when he insisted that every commandment must begin and end with love. Man had learned of love before this God-man came to earth. The Egyptians had tried to love their wives, and Babylonians had been taught to treat each neighbor with dignity and respect. The Jews especially, nourished by the words of Isaias, Ezechiel, and Jeremias, had learned the responsibility of love, and for centuries had struggled to prevent the narrow and arrogant laws of men from smothering the underlying ideal of love. Yet man had not succeeded in loving his fellow man. For every just man there were a dozen pharisees who made a mockery of God by reducing Him to a set of rules imposed on the frightened and defenseless. Thus Jesus would speak of a new commandment, "that you love one another as I have loved you."

And so began the religion of love, to perfect and fulfill the other religions of love that proud men had reduced to the coldness of unyielding law. History had known noble ideals before, but time and fear had wrapped such ideals in the smothering moss of legal codes and tablets. Now Christ, in a manner beyond compare, offered to men a new and thrilling vision. Paul, sparked by such a vision, wrote in a *Letter to the Romans* that man had been "set free from the law" and would be able to live by the sweeping spirit of love.[1] He did not mean that there would be no religious law. He only meant that never again would a man in personal anguish have no recourse but the cold and universal rule that applied to all men. He could be a person because he could know a personal God Who refused to be bound by a single religious rite or the judgmental ruling of a high priest's tongue.

No longer could man reduce the vision of God to the dumb idols that only made permanent the pride and pettiness of man. No longer could man stuff God into the convenient pigeonholes built by men. Now no statue would contain His majesty. No law, or books of law, could prescribe the minute conditions of God's mercy and love. Even Christ, despite the unique possession of the Godhead that was his, could only appear in the simplicity of feet that struggled to walk and hands that tugged impatiently at a mother's breast.

Men could, indeed, call Christ God, even as I do, in simple and indefensible faith. Others might find their God in "Church" or "Abraham" or "personal honesty." But no longer could any man say that he had defined and comprehended God, nor that any other man was certainly without God's forgiving love. God has no name because He has no boundaries, and His love cannot be limited by the blindness or egotism of frightened men.

Yet, despite the efforts of Christ to end religious narrowness, and despite the warnings and reforms of history, I was once a frightened man who sought to contain and package God. I knew the boundaries of His love, the limits of His patience, the very color of His beard. I was, and always will be, a Catholic priest, but I cannot presently be the priest I was. I entered the priesthood with as open and generous a heart as my home and education would allow. I was determined to comfort the sick, to help the poor, to teach children the mysteries of life that I had only begun to live. I was flushed with ideals that promised me I could walk as Christ among the weak. At times I was able to offer His forgiveness, to calm the tragic widow, to encourage the alcoholic, to comfort the skinny adolescent who believed she would never get a date. I taught classes in high school and college, I preached with enthusiasm and preparation, and I knew the quiet and sustaining love the Catholic has for his priest.

Yet daily my anguish grew as I recognized the unholy limits that arrogant and unfounded laws had put on God. I could not walk as Christ because those that needed me most I could not help. The woman who came to me in confession was simply told that she could not practice birth control. There was no chance to tell me that her husband refused to sleep with her unless she took the pill. I did not have to hear of the endless nights when she lay with him, touched him, and felt him pull away. She tried to tell me of her fears that he would find another woman. She tried to describe the way her body ached for him, the memories of a marriage when she nestled warmly in his arms. She wept when she told me how four children under six years of age tore at her patience and how she could not survive without the comfort of her husband. I gave her my answer, I who had never known a baby's voice to interrupt my sleep. I told her that God was asking this noble sacrifice to test her love, that her generosity could never match His own.

It was senseless to talk to me because I had no ears. The pen of a lawgiver had taken them away. Here was a woman who wanted to love her husband, who did not dare to have another child, who gave of herself as I was never asked to do. She was married to a truck driver who was not interested in subtle arguments that told him how he could make love to his wife. He loved her as best he could and she found his love to be the very spark of her own. He loved his children with warmth and manliness, he supported them with the drudgery of daily work. He was giving of himself as much as he was able, and he refused to be intimidated by her scruples about the law of the Church. So she lay with him beneath the sheets in coldness and watched her marriage wither into death.

She came to me as she came to Christ. She came because she knew of nowhere else to go. She came without theology, without an answer for my stilted arguments, with the paralyzing fear that she well might lose the man that drove a truck and fathered her four little ones. And I gave her my theory and my law. I told her that birth control was selfish and unnatural. I told her what I had learned from my textbook and I offered her papal pronouncements to assuage her grief. Even as I told her, I knew that my words were in vain. I secretly hoped that she would return to her man and love him as a woman should, but I knew the guilt that would torture her if she ignored the finality of my words. She was caught in a trap, a careful brainwash that had dissolved her personal experience and left her as a conforming robot before the distant echoes of Roman law.

All she really wanted was to love her husband as Christ had told her she must. She had watched his patience with the children when they puttered with their food or dropped their spoons a thousand times. She had watched him return home from his weary hours on the road. She loved his quiet way, his soft voice, his attentive kindness during each pregnancy. She thought often of her deliveries and the gentle assurance he gave her in her moments of fear and pain. She had a permanent picture of the eyes that thanked her for every child. He was never much with words. He said it with his eyes and the stroke of his hands that soothed her as she lay with him in bed. Now she could love him no longer in the way that he needed to be loved.

The arguments I gave her did not honestly convince me, though long I mouthed them in loyalty, or fear, or misguided faith. She knew more of love than I could ever hope to know, and I, the other Christ, could only make her feel dirty and ashamed. The ideal of Christian love, that she longed to pursue, had been transformed by an angry law into an impossible life. Her marriage well could end, or freeze, or drive her husband to bitterness and neglect. She came to find the Christ who told her that God could never be contained in the chains of impersonal law, and I had ordered her to get in line or give up God.

Don't give me more learned arguments! I have read them all a thousand times.[2] Don't tell me that I must wait patiently for a Pope to appear on a balcony before I can send her home to her husband's bed! I have helped to produce this fearful and imprisoned child who comes helplessly to me. She is not strong enough to walk away as the more sophisticated do daily. She is a victim, a tragedy, a distortion, that I have helped to produce and perpetuate. She has not the intelligence or the courage to defend herself. So she will lose her husband in loyalty to a zealot's law, or ignore that law and join the millions of silent ones who come sheepishly to Mass because I have consigned them "to live in sin."

How did we ever produce the legalistic Church that Christ promised to take away? How did we pass from a gospel of freedom and love to a system that can tear husbands from wives in the name of justice? How did we manage to replace religion with the subtleties of a dead theology? Theology is meant to be a science that tells a man in every age how he can better love his God. It should take the treasures of the gospel and transform them into words and ideas that can tell a modern man how to live and love. Our theology, however, has become a scholar's game. It is a code of rules accumulated in the petty wars of religious bitterness. It is a tale of tired truths, which only serve to rob man of personal responsibility and reduce him to the listlessness of a frightened slave. Theology took away man's mind and left him memorized words. It took away his freedom and robbed him of the romance that should attend his search for God. It dared to enter bedrooms and to tell each man that he must love his wife as does every other man.

This is the theology I learned and transmitted in every confession I heard, every class I taught, every sermon I gave to the guilt-infected flock.[3] I could not preach to free people, I could not suggest, I could only command. I am forbidden to act differently! I must hear confessions as every other priest. I must tell the miserable that they cannot get a divorce—in the name of Christian love. It doesn't matter, the misery that marriage has brought, the bitterness, the vengeance, the distress to children. Obviously I know it all, for I am a Catholic priest. I can tell this woman that God has forbidden her to marry again, and I should know, because I have reduced God to the limits of the system I represent. She can tell me that her second marriage has brought her peace, that her husband has made her more kind and loving than she ever dreamed. He can plead as well, insisting that he loves her children as if they were his own. He can weep before my eyes, as he often does, and I am expected to tell him that this marriage has incurred the wrath of God.

It would be different if I had not studied the sources of such laws, if I did not know the naïve ignorance of the men who are obliged to enforce them. I know, too, the pain of many priests who reject such narrowness as I have described, and have not the tongue or the courage to fight back. Nor do

I have courage. I have only pain. But I refuse to be silent when the helpless sufferers, "the disregarded multitude of the bewildered, the simple and the voiceless" stand naked before the smug arrogance of Catholic law. What a comedy to watch a universal Church await a voice from Rome that will tell them how husbands may sleep with wives. Comedy indeed, if it were not so tragic.

The real tragedy is that Rome does not understand our need. We do not need a solution to the birth-control problem. We need freedom from a system that has taken over our lives.[4] We need freedom from a legalistic Church that has transformed the simplicity of a personal and Christian love into a world of fear and guilt. We do not know how to find God, we have never learned. We have only been taught to keep laws, to avoid sin, to fear hell, to carry a cross that we built ourselves.

I am aware of how the adolescent writhes with guilt when he masturbates. He has been taught by a medieval scholar that he has seriously offended God, that each furtive act in the silence of his room could cast him eternally to hell. I watch him lose all sense of a search for God and become obsessed with his private world of sin and madness. I watch him run to confession in the morning before class. I see him listless in school and I sense that he has known another night of the horror that I have helped to impose. I wonder why he does not hate me. I hide in his conscience on his dates and threaten him with hell if his hand slides curiously over his girl friend's breast. He runs to me to confess, to feel free, to know the warmth of God's forgiveness. Even as I offer him absolution, I well know that I have helped to make him a prisoner for life. I can remember the struggles of my own adolescence, the tense nights when a single memory from a normal day could leave me tortured with the sexual thoughts I had been taught to fear. I can remember my dread of sleep lest death might take me in the night to the court of the God Who sends masturbators to hell. I can remember asking forgiveness a dozen times before I settled into exhausted rest. I can remember the high-school dances when I feared to hold a girl too close lest God would call me in my lust.

No, we do not need a Pope to tell us that Catholics are permitted to use the pill. We need a God to tell us that we are free. We need a Church to deliver us from the legalism that has buried us in guilt and fear and taken away our God. We need a restored faith in ourselves, in the likeness of God that we bear in our bodies and our hearts. We want to learn to love and we have only learned a loyalty to ritual and rules. For years, we ate our fish on Fridays and learned nothing of love in this primitive denial. What kind of man could take such a law seriously? What kind of man could fear to violate this childish command? Yet millions of Catholics are such men, and were as devoted to an outmoded rule as any superstitious savage. How could God possibly care if we eat meat or fish? How could he be bothered with such trivia? And if a man thinks that God is thus concerned, it gives you some idea of that man's view of God.

Somehow, in the passage of kings and castles, we lost our vision of God. Really, it doesn't matter *how*, it only matters that we stand back and look at the rules and rites that have hidden from us our God. The scholars can tell me that He lurks beneath our codes and catechisms, but I will no longer play their game and join them in the search. I can only point to the people I have known as a priest, to the story of my own life, and let the scholars wrestle with their impressive texts. I watch the people at Mass as they read the prayers that do not reach them and struggle to be a community with unfamiliar songs and organized indifference. I listen with them to the sermons that mean less to the preacher than to his flock and watch them squirm at the irrelevance of his words. I watch them come to Mass and wonder why they come. And yet, with sadness I acknowledge that I know why. They come to fulfill a law, they come because they are afraid not to come with the fear that we nourished in them from youth. They come because we demand it, and they have been taught to respect our word as God's own tongue. They come and try each new gimmick that we force upon them to make the Mass more meaningful, and they leave with the same uninspired silence that has become so characteristic of the Catholic flock. They come to find what Christ promised, a community of love and concern, and we give them an auditorium filled with pointless gestures and monotonous words. They come as bodies without heads, faces without names or meaning, to fulfill the law, and they leave as headless and nameless as they came. They ask for God, for meaning, for the strength to give direction to another day, and we greet them with the emptiness of ritual and law.

And yet I cannot blame them for continuing to come. I cannot accuse them of a fear and guilt that I have not shared, a legalism that I have not known. Even as they have given up their search for personal ideals in their servitude before the law, I have permitted my priesthood to become the impersonal ritual and defense of the law that the Church expected. I, who had enough learning to fight, enough awareness to speak out, could only mouth the laws I had learned even as I feared to face the realities of my own life. I could call myself "poor" and continue to share each comfort of the upper middle class. I could bow in priestly "obedience" when I was in reality running from the responsibilities of personal thought. I could enforce laws which made no sense, preach devotions I didn't practice, ask sacrifices I couldn't make, and accept the praise of a people who were fooled by the externals of my life. And yet I kept the rules as they were written, even though they pushed me ever further into myself.

I kept the rule of celibacy in order to free myself to minister to men. I was to be a father to many spirits by denying the fatherhood and pleasures of the flesh. I would be free to care for the sick and lonely, to be available, when other men must chatter with their children or worry with their wife. I was always to be on call, to labor among the bewildered and the poor, to resist temptations to know of love myself. I guarded my thoughts, resisted the offers of love, avoided dangerous involvement, and undertook more projects to occupy my leisure time. Then one day I paused and discovered that I was not celibate at all.

I was a selfish and frightened man who had struggled to keep a senseless law. The celibacy that had promised to make me free, that had meant so much to monks and men of another cast, had only turned me in upon myself and hardened me to love.[5] I had never offered my celibacy to God, I had only kept a rule that shielded me from the involvement that could make of me a man. I had run from the companionship of women in perverted loyalty to a system and a law. I had refused to pause and think, to wonder if my single life had opened me to love. And when I knew, amid the fury of my work and pain, that I would be a better priest with children and a wife, I closed my eyes, turned traitor to my heart, and continued to accept the madness of the law.

Celibacy means misery to me and yet, for years, I was a silent coward, afraid to speak. I knew what a life without marriage had done to me and the hundred priests that revealed to me their heart. I knew our compensations and compromise, I know them now. Thousands of us grow ambitious and aloof, take expensive vacations we do not need, drink far more than we should, become pompous and arrogant, make a parish into a personal kingdom, tease women in the irresponsibility of our boyish charm, grow cold and cynical, make love in childish fantasy, carry noble crosses we build for ourselves, consider the indifference of our flock a personal affront. We are so righteous that we fail to understand weakness, so celibate that we make the sins of sex into the primary target of our religious concern. And yet few of us are celibates.

We are frightened men who keep a rule we do not really understand. We are the victims of a system that absorbed our youthful independence and molded us against our honest will. We have been taught to defend each facet of our faith, no matter our personal feeling, and such an education has made us masters at defending the folly of our legalistic lives. We are prisoners, jailed from the world of free and independent thought, men without authentic choice. We accepted a way of life we did not understand, and continue to embrace its laws because we are robbed of courage to stand alone.

Thus we can pray in Latin when we can barely conjugate, wear vestments that had meaning in another world, fill censers with incense and sprinkle the people with water in archaic and superstitious symbol. And we can be celibates as well, who keep the rules and hope that God will help us in our dilemma and our pain. We are afraid to leave the priesthood, afraid even to alter it, although its legalism has smothered our love. Since we are not even free to leave, it can't be freedom when we stay. Legalism has made us into slaves.

If I were to leave the priesthood because celibacy makes no sense and hides the very Christian love it once was meant to serve, I would be a renegade, a traitor, a man without a home.[6] I would still be a priest, but a wretched and lonely one, adrift from family and from friends. If I were to marry, my parents would be asked to ignore the wife I chose and to shun my children in the name of Christian love. And even though they love me with a deep and filling love, they would not have the freedom to ignore the rulings of the Church. In effect, they would reject me, the son who made them proud and happy, the son who wants to do it still. They would turn away and offer all their misery to God. They would sneak to Church, avoid the pastor, fear each conversation that could whisper of their shame, and wonder where they failed in their labors for my life. But they would reject me, because my arrogant Church has torn away their choice.

And yet I am no celibate who freely gave to God. I am a deluded legalist, who keeps the rules that pay homage to a system and a cause. I am not a celibate because I play a game that I was taught to play. I am a selfish bachelor, a pharisee who speaks of love and only knows of law. I am a man of sophisticated and expensive tastes, a man who never has to get involved, a man more sinful than the ignorant children I condemn, a man insulated from pain and personal concern. My celibacy is an idol, an obsession, a navel-staring worship of myself. I am a man who can ask for money and give to none, gather homage I have never earned, and cherish my body grown too celibate to love.

I see ambition substitute for love, a thirst for titles rob me of my heart.[7] I see my life of narrowness, lack of feeling, the growing inability to care. Celibacy is my shield from reality, my protection from people, the wall that bars me from concern. I am a soldier asked to guard an ancient fort, a sentry who paces with a gun upon a rock. I must not walk among the people lest I hear their anguished cry. I speak from a distance with words that only confuse. The ignorant do not answer me because I do not come too close, or I mouth arguments quite strange to them. And when they do not heed me, I turn my back in smugness and pray for mercy on their soul. I am not a celibate, transformed by service and by love; I am a frightened legalist who made a promise he cannot keep. I have become as helpless as the people whom I lead, as silent as the men who know not how to speak. I am as docile as the truck driver's wife whose contraception I condemned, as fearful as the adolescent who masturbates in guilt, as weary as the Mass-goer who wonders what the Mass means.

I cannot wait for Rome's decisions to change our legalistic ways. I am tired to death of tears I cannot wipe away, of wounds I can only reopen. I can no longer treat the innocent as bricks that feel no pain. I cannot treat men as faceless numbers. I cannot wait for bishops, too frightened and aloof to think, to discuss away our legalism in the comfort of their uninvolved concern. I cannot share their fear that an honest and less decisive Church will confuse and cripple men. I believe that God has touched man too deeply in creation to permit force and terror to make of him a son. Loyalty to law has made us slaves, and I will never more live as a system's serf.

There is no place for persons in our Church.[8] There is only room for groups that nod in blind assent. Each man is asked to accept the Church's stand on birth control, divorce, sex and sin, education and religious life, or if he has the courage to dissent, he is solemnly forbidden to act. I can make no decision in my work unless each syllable has been carefully formed by Rome. I am asked to reject the man who marries a second time, to condemn the single girl who cannot find marriage but knows a life of faithful sex and true, fulfilling love. I must turn from the homosexual or ask of him a promise I know he cannot give. I cannot stand back and help a man to question his ideals, to accept the decision that divorce alone will bring him one step closer to mature and Christian love. I cannot hear the Jewish boy who loves a Catholic girl but who cannot agree to all the smug conditions of my Church. I cannot speak honestly of the obsolete and desperate Catholic schools, of the horror of our convents, of the narrowness of parish life. I cannot experiment, question forms that have lost their meaning, stop hearing confessions that make no sense, unless I seek another way of life. I am not free to marry no matter how ably I might labor as a priest, no matter how selfish I have become without a wife. I am a Catholic, and Catholics must move as a body or cease to know the comforts of the Church. I must wait until each step is clear, and prudent hierarchs have written yet another law.

It is an arrogant Church that knows no way except the way of law. It is a smug Church that can keep a billion children waiting for its word. It is a proud Church that can hold its ears and ignore a million voices raised in pain. It is an unChristian Church that can lose ideals in a multitude of laws. It is a desperate Church that has lost its confidence in men, an angry Church that can bristle and condemn. Yet it is my Church, and I will not walk away in silence and a wounded heart.

If I did not love her, I would not pause to write. If she could not hurt me, I would sneer and move away. But she has formed and fashioned me, nourished and forgiven me, applauded and laughed at me, and presently can break my heart. She can touch my hand, remind me of the priests that have known and loved me, whisper a word about my aging parents, recall the childhood we shared, and I feel sick and hopelessly afraid. I can kneel to her, hold her gently in my young and foolish arms, call her "mother" in hopes that I can be a son. But I cannot be silent when I see her love impoverished into law.

Long enough have I been a priest who forced the simple children against their will. Long enough have I enforced rules in and outside of the confessional which only led men farther from the love of God I sought to bring. I can no longer solve complex stories with the simplicity of law. I can no longer shake my holy fist before the naïve and bewildered soul. Too long have I been the loyal legalist who told children it was against their religion to swim or play basketball at the "Y." I refused the sacraments to the Catholic whose Protestant wife insisted on bringing the children to her Church, denied marriage to the Lutheran who would not raise his children in my faith, forbade non-Catholics to enjoy the dances at our schools, and preached orthodoxy with the fury of a man gone mad. Young men apologized to me when they dated non-Catholics and girls wept to me when I would not marry them to their agnostic fiancés in our Church.

The spirit of legalism, learned in my parochial school and molded in my seminary life, touched every phase of my priestly life. It infected my confessions, leaked through all of my classes, and bathed the whole of my pastoral work. The Church was always right, her critics were ignorant and seething with prejudice and hate. I fought the social workers who believed in birth control among the poor, and bragged about it over Scotch and steak. I condemned the hospitals which permitted abortion or sterilization, the doctors who suggested that mothers should have no more children, the professors who spoke of the intolerance of the Church. I did all of this in the name of law, a law which could ignore exception or discussion.

But now I have had enough. I can neither be silent nor a legalist any longer. I cannot accept this simplistic view of man and life. I can no longer force Catholics, blackmail Protestants, scorn Jews, or uphold Catholic ways which are ridiculous and obsolete. I can no longer deny the sacraments to anyone who asks for them. I can no longer hear confessions with an un-yielding eye held on the law, nor refuse burial to anyone who has requested such. I cannot live without mercy and personal love, nor cease to do the true work of a priest. I cannot be a mere judge and jailer, a ritualist and a mouther of tired words, a defender of a tradition which must reform or die. So I will protest with words that are written in the memory of the sense-less suffering I have known and seen, and this book is the account of that anguished protest.

Some men, despite the law, have become free in the midst of the system that reduced the rest of us to helpless pain. These men, however, are the noble exception who prove that there once lurked God beneath the law. They are the hope that man will survive the corruptions that made us prisoners even as it promised to make us free. They are the few men of courage who could walk alone without the gentle guidance of the Church. They had the wisdom to pick and choose, the joy to distinguish the rind from the fruit. The rest of us are not as gifted or as brave. We cannot stand alone without the Church that taught us to depend.

We know we need some law, as every family does, but we also know that the thickness of our legal code is proportionate to the absence of confidence and love. The man who must ever resort to the law to hold us is the man afraid of us, be-cause he is first afraid of himself. He does not trust man, nor believe in his nobility, nor sense the Creator's mark that rests on him. The fiercest confessor is the man who is nearest to sin. The most severe legalist is the man who is closest to sever-ing the law. He does not trust his own humanity and this is to admit a world's defeat. Only a loving father can give a child a goal and give him the freedom to pursue it. Only a genuine family can trust a child enough to make of him a man. Only a home can offer its children the chance to be wrong in order that they may know the joy of being right.

2. THE MAN WHO IS

A PRIEST

I was a legalist, born in a happy ghetto, and the history of my formation explains the leadership of my Church. Mine was not the ghetto of Boston or New York, where Catholics crowded together with beer and stick ball and elected Democrats as defenders of the faith. Mine was the ghetto of a lonely Catholic family in a neighborhood of ambitious WASPs.* Yet in essence it was the same—except that I had to travel farther to Church and school to know the security of my group. Once settled among people of my own kind, I knew the special joys that only a happy ghetto could give.

My parents had only dreamed of college, and went to work early to repay their own impoverished parents for the gift of life. They were intelligent, strong and disciplined, ambitious and afraid. The ghetto taught them to fear hell, to mistrust the rich and the products of state universities, to be in awe of the pastor, to be concerned with what others might think, and to live as if the present world really didn't count. I shared their fears, inherited their drive and ambition, admired their loyalty and sacrifice, adopted their anger and prejudice, knew the fierceness of their love and hopes, developed their capacity for hard work, and learned in their ghetto world of blacks and whites.

* White Anglo-Saxon Protestants.

We lived in a world without grays, as the Church carefully taught. It is the only world in which a ghetto can survive. I fought for my existence among ghettos equally as impervious and afraid: the Masons, who told us we were not Americans; the Jews, who spoke of persecution and secretly sought revenge; the WASPs, who laughed at the mounting laundry on our Monday lines and didn't believe their own blood was red; the Christian Reformed, who called starch and dour faces the mark of sanctity; and the Methodists, who got sin confused with bad posture and dirty fingernails.

We did not ignore our neighbors; we smiled and knew their names. We played football with their boys and teased their screaming girls, but we knew that they could never be as strong and pleasing to God as we. I learned in school that I was more proficient in the wisdom of the soul, that I must give a good example to those less fortunate than I. Above all, I knew that I could not date a Protestant or, especially, marry one.

The heroes of my world were the priests and sisters, more important than doctors or presidents, more wise than scholars or diplomats, more worthy of respect than police or even parents.[1] Their decisions were clear and final, and could invade each facet of my life. When I was caught kissing with seventh-grade passion, I was solemnly turned over to the priest. When I skipped school, I was sent to the enraged pastor. In my school, Lincoln's birthday was outranked by the pastor's own. I greeted the priest each time he passed, tipped my hat to him in winter, and opened doors for him all year long. I could not criticize his sermons, question his actions, nor even mention his name without charity or praise. If he drank and showed the effects, he obviously had a cold. If he snarled about sex or money, he was nervous and working too hard. I was not to talk back; I was to be grateful for criticism, and never to refuse the most impossible request.

I learned my religion without question and memorized each answer without complaint.[2] I knew the angels by name and size, and could prove the authority of the Church. Luther was a renegade who lost his faith, Calvin a troubled man who gave in to angry pride. I knew how fortunate I was to be a Catholic, how special in God's eyes I must be. God, however, began to look more like a Roman collar who heard confessions and said the Mass.

I never thought about attending the public school, steeped as it was in worldliness and sin. But the choice was never mine or my parents' to make. To attend a public school was to be cast among the wolves, to be disgraced within the ghetto as one too slow or stubborn to be taught. It was to study in a world where I could not learn of God or take the time to pray. I was lucky to be in a Catholic school, I learned, and often heard how generous were my parents and pastor to build me such a shrine.

I was proud of my school, and proud that I knew the comforts of my faith. Daily Mass was the first "class" of my day, and confession the last "exercise" on Friday afternoon. I gave up candy and movies during Lent, wore my scapular medal to bed as well as in the bath, said my rosary regularly, prayed at morning and at night, kept track of each sin of disobedience or unkind speech. I prayed for my vocation every day, and served at Mass from second grade.

I admired the priest with genuine respect. He was the biggest man in my life, and to please him was the secret target of my hopes. His approval made my day, his request for service was an honor, his visit to our home a triumph beyond all words. I watched my mother prepare his favorite food, my father lament the vastness of a priest's work, and the family grin with fondness and unaccustomed joy. I watched the attention each one gave his words, the majesty with which he spoke, the confidence with which he dispatched the unbelievers of the world. I saw the envy of the Catholic neighbors who watched him leave our home—and I knew that I would one day be a priest.

So, at fifteen years of age, when World War II was almost at an end, I left for the seminary. It was a hard decision to leave my home. It meant an end to freedom, a painful sacrifice of my chance to play quarterback, and a sad farewell to the first little dark-haired girl who tripped my heart. I will never forget the day we drove away from home. I felt I was leaving the world and in a peculiar way I was. I would return for vacations, spend the summer building houses or pumping gas, play golf with my brothers, or swim until our eyes were bloodshot and our appetites fierce. But I would never be the same again, since I had decided to be a priest. I was never to date, was to avoid movies, beaches, and mixed parties, and to attend Mass every day, meditate each morning of my life, and select a summer job which would not jeopardize my special call. I kept each rule as scrupulously as it was written and explained. My father told me I was too serious, my mother said that I had lost my personality and spark. There were explosions in the summer when the tension ran too high. There were frequent doubts about my choice, but I knew I had to be a priest. I had been "called," and I could not refuse the request that came from God. I was a hero in the ghetto when I returned home for vacation, armed with a black suit and tie, a bulky Latin missal.

I was exempted from the service by the importance of my work and felt cowardly and less a man when I talked to former classmates in the Army or Marines. But the pastor now invited me to his home, the sisters greeted me with new respect, and even my parents could not hide the special place they saved for me within their hearts. I was a seminarian, a chosen man, the pride of the parish, the future leader of our Church. And I was indescribably alone.

I, who once had been the center of every laughing group, the restless boy who could not wait for morning's light, was suddenly alone. I was in the world, but not of it; I was unique, untouchable, aloof, the special friend of God. And year by year, I learned to live alone. My parents could not reach me any more, my brothers could not share with me their dealings and their dates. I learned to fear the world, to hide from its social life, and gradually my solitary life was more the fruit of my warped psychology than of my devotion and sacrifice.

I even began to find vacations far too long and returned to the seminary with relief. Here every decision was made for me, and I was shielded from the fleeting pleasures of the world. I could not leave the grounds, see a girl, read a magazine, drive a car, escape the iron discipline that bound me in its arms. And when I faltered, the voices were always there to tell me I was different, unlike the rest of men: the hope of the world, the strength of the sinner, the lonely man who gave his life for all. I learned to see the world as sinister and dark, and I would be the feeble burst of life. I was called a man, a child of flesh and blood, a weak and sinful child like all of Adam's own—but I knew that I was set apart and chosen from the herd.

I was a seminarian and I cannot tell you what it meant. I cannot, with memory's help, tell you whether I was happy or sad, triumphant or troubled, longing to go on or afraid to give up. I only know that I returned to the seminary year by year and ceased to be a man. I was a prophet, a hero, a soldier, a trained mind, a judge, a reformer, a contradiction, an ascetic, another Christ, an island, a crusader, but not a man. I could never again be ordinary, doubtful, carnal, or confused. I do not know what drove me, whether God, or man's respect, idealism, personal choice, or fear of hell. I only know I struggled on and ended up a priest.

My education was difficult. I studied Latin and Greek, French and Hebrew, English, Philosophy, Speech, Theology, History, Science, and Math. I studied four years after college until I was declared ready to be a priest. My studies spoke seldom of doubts or opinions and most frequently of blacks and whites. In philosophy, for example, we could handle Berkeley, Hume, and Kant in a single week. John Locke was seen as patently confused and Nietzsche was an angry cynic with nothing of consequence to say. We memorized each thesis and definition and proved that "reason" could only lead an honest man to faith. We were the only honest men as we defended by "reason" all the moral teachings of the Church. Catholic opposition to divorce and birth control, to freedom of speech and thought, to mercy killing and adultery were all the obvious conclusions of a "reason" unclouded by passion and pride. It did not seem important that there were millions of "unreasonable" men. I still lived in a ghetto, a child's playground, where I could ignore anyone who refused to play according to my rules.[3]

It was an education without sympathy, a training without recourse. I heard what I was supposed to hear, and said what the administration expected me to say. Rebels were weeded out. Only the strong and legal-minded, or the naïve and passive, could last. Creativity was discouraged unless it pursued the accepted patterns which cautious minds approved. "Heresy" was a word which ended every argument, and "the Church teaches" was the narrow outline of every debate. I was not educated, I was formed. I was not encouraged to think, but trained to defend. I was not asked to reflect, but to memorize.

Even the final four years after college, the years set apart for the "advanced" study of theology, were no different. Only the devoted men who taught me made it possible to survive. I learned what I was expected to believe of heaven and hell, angels and men, even the mysterious God. The truths were laid out in cube form. The heretics who questioned Rome were peremptorily embalmed with a papal decree or conciliar attack. It was a peculiar kind of mathematics, but never a study of man and God. I studied the thousands of sins that had been gathered in the mire of a million confessions. I started with the presumptions that others demanded of me, and if I questioned them, I was asked to abandon the game.

Even the Scriptures were reduced to a defense of the Catholic Church. We read John to defend confession, Luke and Paul to forbid divorce. Even purgatory received its vague, unquestioned scriptural support. After a time I was able to see anything as proved from anything as long as my conclusions supported the Church. Then I could call myself a "theologian," a scholar, who could keep the mud from the sanctuary of the Church. I could no longer go nakedly to Scripture and walk in the wonder of its simple love.

It was also during these last four years that I was immersed in the 2400 laws or "canons" which control the Catholic

Church. The canons are the cryptic conclusions of scholars and religious lawyers long since dead—bastard laws, without apparent forebears, arranged side by side with the decrees of common sense. There are the rules for Christian burial in consecrated ground, the penalties for abortion and suicide, laws regulating the powers of the bishop, the duty of preaching, the sins whose forgiveness is reserved to the Pope. It is an archaic body of law, reeking of drawbridges and moats, which has long impeded the spontaneity of Catholic thought.[4] Canon law has always had the last word in the Church, and it can censor books or excommunicate men with the power of an atomic guillotine.[5] The nervous fingers of bishops can point to it when rebels threaten the complacency of the Church. I learned the laws and read the commentaries and was too frightened to wonder what had happened to the freedom that is Christ.

After such a training I was ready to labor as a priest. I had taken no courses in psychology or counseling. I knew nothing of man's true temptations nor the limits of his capacity to obey. I had never really lived, nor felt, nor hurt as other men. I was ready to enforce the law, and the narrowness of my training ensured the prospering of the Catholic world of black and white. I knew the laws and would teach them with vigor and unquestioned loyalty. I was still the same callow boy who had bowed to the pastor and kissed the confirming bishop's ring. Only my confidence and vocabulary had grown. I still had the ghetto mind, now fortified by formula and law. I was blind to the Church's weakness, I admired its strength. I could call a lack of feeling "courage," stubbornness "conviction," blindness "tradition," medieval prejudice "the unchanging law of Christ." I could explain away failure as success, any fault as evidence of strength, and injustice or cruelty as the modern expression of "God's will." And in such blind and narrow prejudice, I was desperately sincere.

So I took my place in the clergy as another Catholic priest. I would tell men how to love though I had never even kissed. I would chide the young lovers, warn the adolescent, threaten the husbands who used contraceptives, laud Catholic schools

from the pinnacle of my ignorance, refuse sacraments to the
lonely divorced, nag for money from the economically op-
pressed, demand sacrifices of the single I could not make
myself, command Lutherans to raise their children Catholic,
condemn Masonry for obsolete reasons, attack a world I only
feared and never knew.

And in my new-found position of power I accepted the
homage of the docile Catholic and ignored the hatred of those
scorned and wounded by the Church. I did not question my
leaders or my laws. I kept the first commandment of every
bishop: "Thou shalt not rock the boat!"[6] Most boat-rockers
are weeded out before ordination and only occasionally does a
man of original and independent thought slip through. Soon
enough are they silenced. The conservatives are the fabric that
makes up the wardrobe of the Church. They are the young
monsignors with the confident smiles and ambitious eyes. They
are the bishops who have earned their purple by their uninvolved devotion to law. They are the men who can keep and
make the rules because they have guarded their hearts from
honest dialogue with men. They force the independent into
line, talk more of money than of men, and equate progress
with an absence of tension and unrest. From such a group there
can never come a Bishop Pike, hardly a Monsignor Pike, and
only until the word gets out can a Father Pike come. Yet herein
are bred the leaders of the Catholic Church, who can debate
the wisdom of the Friday fast when modern man is pondering
the death of God.

I am no conservative, nor is my bishop apt to solicit my
advice. Yet I have lived and worked as blindly as all the rest.
I am a priest, and to be such is to be well guarded from the
complexity that is truth. Not only has my education narrowed
my mind into little cubes which reject or distort any information that is new, but my relationships with people are frequently insincere. People call me "Father" and they pay me
no compliment. They stand aloof from me, they agree and
grin, when deep within their hidden anger they would like to
slap my face.

I am never "Jim," I am the patriarchal "Father," the man who sees but half of life and seldom hears the truth. People have been taught to fear me, to cater to me, to make few demands, to give me the benefit of the doubt. If I enter a room full of strangers, I am the center of attraction without ever knowing the struggles of ordinary men. Sweet ladies hand me coffee and cookies, men laugh heartily at my slightest joke. They clean up their stories, bore me with the memories of priests they have formerly known, nod seriously when I smother them with clichés. I can preach badly and make no effort to solve man's problem or reach his heart, and poor deluded fools will praise me for my words. Even the more intelligent are apt to excuse my meaningless words with pity for the abundance of my work. Yet I was not too busy to preach well—I was watching the late movie and sipping Scotch. If I told them this, they would call me "humble" in their stubborn refusal to see me as a man.

I am not "Jim"; I am a giant, the collected myth of the centuries, the arrogant and opinionated talking machine that beguiles and frightens men. They speak to me and seldom can I trust their words. They have been taught how they must speak to one as untouchable as I. They pamper me, baby me, caress me with the words that tell me I'm a "thing." They see my collar, my smug confidence, my centuries of angry tradition. They never see the fear that trembles within me, the doubt that lies buried in my heart. If they swear, they apologize. If they talk of sex, they garnish it with fig leaves and flowers.

I watch the gentle scrubwoman who cleans offices at night. Her husband drinks and rapes her once a month. She has seven children, each more delinquent than the next. She should have left her husband twenty years ago. She has stayed with him because "Father" told her it was best. She had the children because she couldn't practice birth control. She confesses minutely each secret thought of sex. She worries endlessly that God has cut her off. She comes to my office clutching her offering for a Mass and whispers her request. I take her money, throw a crumb of kindness to her fond, adoring eyes, and she kisses my priestly hand as she apologizes for taking up my time.

I am "Father," the man who never has to know the misery that is man. No question puzzles me, no moral dilemma puts me off. The man who talks back to me is proud, the sinner who quarrels with me is unrepentant and obstinate. I am always right, always deserving of respect. My faults are excused, my ignorance overlooked, my immaturity condoned. I sit in a restaurant and men who do not know me pay my bill. They send me drinks, slap my back, extoll my sacrifice, praise my school, quote my words. They do everything but treat me as a man.

They do not understand me, they do not even want to try. They do not know that I drink and lust like all the rest. They do not realize that the lewdest jokes are told me by priests. They smile at me with a smile I never earned. They respect my intellect when it has pondered nothing but the sports page for years. They give me their attention and acquiescence when they should argue with me, question me, strip off their shirts and show me their wounds. But they smile, and call me "Father," and treat me as a history's skeleton.

They do not react to me, they react to the illusion they have created in my place. When they tell me they love me, I cannot believe them. They love me for the forgiveness I give, forgiveness of sins that I have invented. They love me for the rituals I perform, the rituals I give meaning by my parroted words. They love me for the fear I calm, the fear I created by my terrifying vision of sin. They love me for the few sparks of humanity that my cassock cannot filter out. They love me with the love born of superstition and magic, the love I cannot earn or honestly deserve. And so they call me "Father" when I know I'm only "Jim."

I cannot trust their love because they do not speak their hate. They hold it in, swallow it, and smother it with that ever-present smile. If at times they would defy me, challenge my words, dissipate my certitude, mock my arrogance, question my infallibility, then I could know their love. If they could come to me as "Jim," a priest, and not to the impersonal "Father" who lives without freedom of decision and must treat every sin alike, then I could know when they loved me and when they only smiled because they were not free to hate.

I am a priest, a bully, a mouther of words, a man whose training forbids him to trust his heart. I cannot say, "Go in Peace," or "Much is forgiven because much you have loved." Rather, I must quote the law like a scheming coroner who runs a mortuary on the side. I see each sin in a paragraph and not immersed in the anguish of a searching soul. And after a dozen years of work among a smiling, docile people, I must pause and wonder who I am. I do not know if I am kind or beastly, open or narrow, strong or weak, faithful or comfortable, courageous or naïve, generous or selfish, because Catholics cannot react to me as a man.

Don't call me "Father." Call me "Jim," and make me know the reality that is life. Don't agree with the obsolete conclusions that I have memorized from musty books. Don't sit and listen to the pious irrelevance that I hand you in place of Christ. You have made me a witch doctor, a magician with secret potions and strange, esoteric words. Why can't I tell you of my fears and personal doubts? Why can't I share with you my weakness when you struggle with your own? Why can't I say, "Do what you think is best," rather than bully and frighten you with neat conclusions that neither you nor I have reached?

You have made me proud and arrogant with the docility of your smile. I do not have to search for new answers, for new approaches and insights, since you patiently accept the irrelevance I hand you from the past. You come to Mass and I bore you, but you bow and come again. You come to confession and I lecture you, but you thank me and promise to return. You don't need me, you only need an impersonal specter robed in black. You won't let me be myself, you permit me to be a tradition, a voice as dull and domineering as all the rest. What have you done to me? What have I become?

No man can take the unquestioned obedience you give and long remain a man. No wonder I think myself infallible when you treat me as the unerring custodian of truth. No wonder I have grown smug and arrogant, righteous and unfeeling, when you have not loved me enough to disagree. I am not a man, but only a seminarian grown to man's estate.

My God! What have I become? You asked me to minister with the weakness of my flesh, to serve the struggling sinner, and I have grown rigid and comfortable in the service of myself. I am not "another Christ," I am not even a man. I am only a prisoner, a synthetic paragon, a defender of the tired past.

O weak and wounded people, how often I long to comfort you with other words than law. How often I want to whisper that my God will understand. But I can only send you back to misery and to guilt and promise a misty happiness that follows after death. I know how you suffer and I grow bitter and angry in your pain. I am a doctor who offers leeches and bloodletting for your fever, because I fear to operate. I am an old lady who tells you how much fun I had in days forever lost. I am a statesman in his dotage who speaks of a world long since gone. I am obsolete, irrelevant, afraid.

O God, if I am to be a priest, first let me be a man! Do not let me hide behind my collar, my titles, my false front. Do not make me give answers I do not believe, nor mold men into impersonal and uncomplaining dolts. Let them know my doubts from my own lips, and let them tell me honestly of theirs. Let me not bind them with law and hell, nor frighten them with tales of unexpected death.

I know their struggles, their differences, the uneven patterns of their lives. It was You, God, Who made them different, and I who ask them all to be the same.[7] Let them know the romance of the search for You, the doubts and near despair that mark the path of honest men. Let me serve them in a personal way and not in the dispassionate sameness that has colored all my work. Let me root out conformity and offer faith, tear down compliance and build up love, eradicate guilt and produce unfailing hope. Let them see my manhood that they may pay homage to their own. Then I can be a priest and not the indentured slave of a system bound in upon itself.

One Sunday, while traveling, I stopped to assist at Mass in a neat suburban Church. I was distressed, fighting with simple fears that I knew I must resolve. I went to Church, not expecting a sudden solution, but hoping for a word that might provide the courage to live another day. I wanted someone to tell me that I was not all bad, that I was only human like the rest of men. The priest ascended the altar and I liked his young and gentle way. He seemed quiet, humble, a man. I fumbled with my own thoughts and waited for him to speak. He told me that the world was selfish, that the collections were down, that the people were not singing well at Mass. He whined of the sufferings of the friends we had in purgatory and shamed us that we had forgotten them so soon. He quoted Scripture to enforce his views on suffering after death, and bored me with the dullness of his words. Then he asked us all to stand and say the Creed.

I could not pray with him, I could only pity the ignorance he displayed. I wanted to stand up and shout, to lead a mob and tear the vestments from his back. I wanted to drag him from his pulpit and lead him to the world of men. I wanted him to walk among the lonely and the poor, to eat with them, to weep with them, to laugh and drink a beer with them. I wanted him to throw away his books and look at men, to look into the eyes of those who did not run from life. I wanted to tear off his collar and make him wear a tie, to send him to an anonymous job to buy his children bread. I wanted him to sweat over income tax, to experience the loneliness of the bewildered, the horror of living with a wife he did not love. I wanted him to bear another child when he could ill afford the three he had, to eat with infants, to lose a job, to make a friend, to be scorned and overlooked.

I wanted him to commit adultery, to masturbate in growing frustration, to fight with his wife, to drink too much, to think of suicide, and then to line up and confess his sins to an arrogant Catholic priest. Then I would lead him back to the pulpit, back to his vestments and lace, and I would listen to his words, and watch his human face. And maybe I would begin to see a man, and to respect him as a priest. Maybe then I could call him "Father" and mean it from my heart. But that Sunday I could only call him "boy" and ache and wonder when he and I could serve as Catholic priests—and still be men.

3. THE MAN WHO IS A CATHOLIC

Some years ago, when I was a young curate, the Notre Dame football team came to Lansing, Michigan, to challenge the Spartans of Michigan State. The team chaplain visited our rectory the night before the game and announced that the squad would like to attend Mass at nine o'clock on the morning of the clash. He asked if I would help with communions and confessions for the fifty crusaders who came from South Bend to give glory to Erin and its God. I, a Notre Dame fan of considerable strength, was more than willing to be on hand. It was Paul Hornung's senior year and Aubrey Lewis, a great runner, was beginning to come to prominence.

After the Mass, the chaplain and I watched the players file to the front of the Church and kneel solemnly at the communion rail. They knelt as warriors, knights of Mary and the Church, the solemn heroes of Catholic education. They received a special blessing, a tiny medallion in their outstretched palms, and honored a relic of the true Cross. Their faces were drawn and serious, Hornung himself was flushed, as we passed by and brought them the protection of the heavenly patrons of an autumn afternoon. This was our secret weapon, the added strength unknown to television and the press. Unfortunately, however, the Spartans didn't get the word and Notre Dame went down to a decisive and inglorious defeat.

Years later, I took a trip to Lourdes in southern France. I stood in the giant square in front of the Basilica and watched the Catholics of the world await the special blessing of this sacred shrine. I was jostled by the Italian ladies in their shawls, distracted by Eastern Europeans who whispered their prayers out loud. I watched the sick on their litters, the American businessmen in their clean white shirts. I saw priests wrapped in the cassocks of the world, excited Africans in their multicolored native garb. But most of all I saw the wrinkled faces, speaking out the sincerity of their pain. They had come to ask a favor, like the Moslem hordes at Mecca, and to know a special contact with their God. They drank the water there, which is noted for its miraculous effects. They bought the plastic bottles to bring the water home. They bought rosaries and medals by the basketful and had them blessed by the pudgy hands of sweating priests. They covered the grounds like locusts, bent on devouring each shred of special grace. They kissed the feet of statues and groaned in mildewed shrines. They confessed in every language and munched their mountain cheese. Then, like a giant, contented herd, they went home to bed. And so did I, as sick and confused by superstition as I had been on that autumn day when the Spartans conquered Rome.

Not only was I sick and confused, I was deeply ashamed as well. This was my Church and these were the Catholic men I had helped to form, the statistics we added up when we counted the catholicity of our Church. My mind was crowded with thoughts that refused to let me sleep. I thought of a temple court in Jerusalem when an angry Jesus cast the hucksters out. I thought of a Moses who stormed down a mountain and made powder of a golden calf. Then I thought of the frightened Catholics who worried and prayed in every parish I had served. I thought of the man who is a Catholic and I think of him once again.

The Catholic man sees the world through a system which forbids him to be himself. He can walk the city streets and watch every face and every situation fall neatly into its proper category. He has never really known the joy of search, the wonder of discovery, the exciting freedom of personal decision. The world is a stranger to him since he judges its citizens before he really knows and understands. He has been taught what to read, how to think, and whom to call his friend.

I watch the Catholic come to Mass and pity the formation that warped his mind and distorted his religious sense. He comes because he has been told to come by religious leaders who are as docile and listless as he. He reads the prayers wrapped in stilted phrases and makes the gestures totally foreign to his modern way of life. He lives in a world of jets and atomic bombs, and prays in a world of medieval magic. He is bored in the presence of his God. And yet he comes, because he has learned from his youth that hell is the home of those who miss Mass. He is too frightened to admit he is bored.

In his business his eye is tuned to efficiency and progress. He looks for shortcuts, for new ways to reach the public, for another service that will attract his fellow man. He has views on world peace, opinions on fiscal reform, thoughts on crime prevention, mental health, and transportation in megalopolis. But in religion he is a robot who can only recite the answers he has learned. He will accept the priestly decisions without protest, appear thoughtful when he hears a rehash of the truths he learned in school, and support the Church which has robbed him of his mind.

And his wife is as pitiful as he. She will live in guilt, raise her children in superstition and fear, and thank the Church for the delicate blueprint that prevents her growth. She will oppose abortion and sterilization without really knowing why. She will practice rhythm or abstinence to win martyrdom in her husband's bed. She will have another child when she neglects the handful that she has, and if she is finally abused enough to protest, she will be stilled by the gentle accents of the priest or be forced to walk away. I remember the mother who came to complain that I had taken away her husband by the papal rules I had enforced. He was sleeping with his secretary once or twice a week, because she, his wife, was too terrified to risk a pregnancy, and too brainwashed to practice birth control. She had returned to her parents' home with her four children, was taking tranquilizers every few hours, and lately had thought of suicide. Her doctor had sent her to me, suggesting that I might give her some secret permission to be a woman once again. She and I talked for an hour, reflecting on the mysterious ways of God. I told her of the holy women of the past, of Mary beneath the Cross, of the sainted martyrs of our parish Church. She grew calm, determined, guilty, courageous, ready to do God's will and bear her cross. She thanked me amid her tears, returned to her parents' home, and four months later joined another Church.

Indeed, she had sense enough to leave before she lost her mind. But can she live with the guilt and fear that we taught her from her earliest years? Can she feel a pain in her chest without wondering if God will suddenly welcome her to hell? Can she bear to pass a Church, or see a priest, or read a newspaper without feeling that she has done a crime? Will she ever love her husband without guilt? Will she lie awake when he is sound asleep? She didn't really leave her Church; we pushed her out, and such conversions do not lead to peace.

The man or woman who is a Catholic has lost his touch with life. He is afraid to read the books that others read, to see the movies that reflect our modern life. He is told that *Dear John*, a current movie, is harmful to his moral life, and he accepts this decision. I saw it, and found it more meaningful than *The Song of Bernadette*. It speaks eloquently of the simplicity of human love and reaches man where his sophistication meets his soul. It is more "religious" than most sermons heard in a Catholic Church, more meaningful than the trappings of the Mass. It is adult, worldly, true, poignant, painful, and sad—and forbidden to Catholics. The Catholic is not supposed to reflect on man and woman making love. He is not expected to explore the world in which he daily lives. He is asked to ignore it, to hide from it, to run from temptation, as if God were somewhere else than at the core of man's own soul.

The Church, like a frightened and angry parent, takes too

much credit for the help that it can offer man. Consequently, Catholics are treated as children and they continue to behave as such.[1] They confess their sexual affairs when they should pause and examine them. They call a loveless marriage virtue if it doesn't break the rules. They call a personal friendship sinful even if single adults grow mature enough to love within this close relationship. They offer solutions before they have examined the problem, give answers before they are informed enough to speak. They condemn family planning in India or Japan without awareness of the culture of the East. They do not reach decisions, they mimic the words that other men provide.

They made a saint of Franco without pausing to hear the other side. They supported the insanity of McCarthyism despite the protests of more balanced men. They approach every social question with a handful of principles that other minds have formed. They support Catholic education with arguments that have lost their force. If time tells them they were wrong, they refuse to apologize. The Catholic man is a little boy whose mommy tells him how to think. God is on his side and the power of God's Spirit rests within his Church. His defenses are made of steel, and he has given his arrogant solutions so often that he is convinced of them himself.

The Catholic man opposed evolution and he was wrong. He supported monarchy long after democracy had made the people free. He promoted racial prejudice until "pagans" showed him he was wrong. He fought mixed marriages and fights them still, although he enjoys the freedoms that pluralism has won. He asks for freedom of conscience and expects Protestants to raise their children in his faith. He condemned Stevenson and Rockefeller because they were divorced. He praised Kennedy because he was Catholic, and extolled Johnson because his daughter chose the Catholic Church. He takes credit for the athletes who go to Mass, selects a Catholic All American Team, and wonders how a Catholic football star could matriculate at Michigan State.

He still believes that the world will be Catholic before the judgment comes, that his faith is a mark of special love from God, that death will justify the valor of his choice. His priests are chosen men, while rabbis and ministers are ambitious, prejudiced, or misinformed. He sees his monks and nuns as proof of God's Shadow on the Church, and the Buddhist counterparts as deluded fanatics.[2] He is the man of the clear-eyed and simplistic look. No problem is complex, no position doubtful, no moral dilemma beyond the papal grasp. If the Pope will permit the pill, the Catholic attitude will simply be reversed. The Catholic will then defend the pill, make light of its physical effects, command its use as the holy will of God. Until it is approved, he will not move because he has learned to watch and wait. He has not the right to follow his own conscience, or the power to select the principles that give him help. He is a Catholic, a child, who demands that another make for him his choice.

He has nothing to learn from Lutherans, no wisdom to be gained from Jews, Masons are a mob of greedy and vengeful men who love to persecute the Church. Atheists are proud and selfish, agnostics educated beyond their brains. Scientists are suspect unless they join the Church, doctors are proud and dangerous unless they listen to the Pope. Thus, the Catholic man cannot truly know the meaning of dialogue, but only give arguments to defend the position he has inherited from his youth. His back is up before his mind begins to work, and he has his defenses well laid before his brother has had a chance to speak.

The Catholic man is an organized answering service whose first obligation is to protect his Church. He is not concerned with overpopulation, but only with guarding the Catholic position on the pill. He is not troubled about public education, but only about the growth of Catholic schools. He seldom spends time with programs of mental health or housing or city government, unless some Catholic value will ultimately thrive. Thus, in every social reform Catholic support has always been joined to the caboose. The Catholic did not support the Negro until the cause was popular and safe. He dared not rethink his views on Communism until our whole society suggested such a change. He did not battle for justice in the coal mines, or start a war on poverty, or strive for women's equal rights. He is a joiner, a sycophant, a man who marches to commemorate battles he has not fought. He cannot go out on a limb, he cannot risk his reputation, he cannot be a radical—he must bide his time and wait patiently for the priest.

And he waits still. The Catholic fears to be a pacifist until "Father" tells him that he may. His stand on Red China, or on Vietnam, will reflect the conservatism of his Church. He lives in a world without surprises, a world that resists experiment and change. He cannot take another look, for example, at homosexuality and wonder if the traditional moral position is realistic or sound. He will continue to condemn abortion even if the law approves it state by state. He will resist divorce until his extremism makes him the laughingstock of the world. He will close his eyes and stuff his ears and thank God he is shielded from the world.

He will come to "Father" and ask questions that do not require the answers of a priest. Parents will ask when teenagers should date, when evening curfew should come, when a boy should be allowed to drive a car. The young will ask how long an engagement should last, or wonder if they can attend a synagogue or wear a bikini on the beach. Workmen will ask if they can bowl in the Masonic temple, women will ask if they can trade in a drugstore that sells suggestive books, or if children can watch Walt Disney in a theater that showed The Doll and Jules and Jim, or swim at the YMCA.

The man who is a Catholic is a religious child who cannot make a moral decision without priestly support. This is especially true of anything that pertains to sex. The Catholic is obsessed with sex and the least deviation can leave him frantic until he finds a priest. He will hurry to confession to clear his eyes of miniskirts, to free his ears from dirty jokes. He will be guilty if his eyes rest on a rounded breast or gaze too longingly at swaying hips. Sex is the chief and single sin, man's fleshly battle with the world.

Sex is the target of the Catholic conscience, the preoccupation of the Catholic adolescent no matter what his age. It leers from billboards and hounds the Catholic on the beach or in his bed. I hear about it from the old men in rest homes who sometimes touch their withered flesh to test its life. I hear it from the children in their simple confessions when they whisper of the explorations held in some garage. It shouts at me from every confession, covers me with questions and detail. Each week I swim in hands and thighs, back seats and bedrooms, trembling lips and throbbing breasts. I hear the embarrassed voices of the weak and wonder if the Catholic thinks of anything but sex. And I know that its expressions cannot be so serious if its occurrence is as frequent as it seems.

Perhaps you are among the educated and independent and do not recognize the Catholic I describe. Perhaps you are a liberated Catholic, or your friends are, and you do not know the suffering of the millions bound by Rome. I know them, and I cannot forget their weariness and fear. I cannot leave them prisoners while I enjoy the freedom that my temperament and education can provide. Were I married, I could practice birth control without concern. Indulgences bore me and I have not tried to gather them for years. I do not pray to angels nor honor history's saints. I know nothing of heaven nor do I really fear the misery of hell. I do not run to confession, nor sprinkle holy water, nor seek from novenas what only time and effort give. I do not wait to hear each sentence from the Vatican before I act, nor do I fear the excommunications sent in solemn words. I will not accept the bishops' fears and arrogant commands as the unerring voice of God, nor permit ignorant pastors to transform their petulance into law.

But I am not the average Catholic man, who cannot escape the shackles and superstitions of his past. He cannot ignore the laws that have lost their meaning, or distinguish the mysteries from myth.[3] He is choked by sin, frightened by the fire of hell, and bound by the hierarchy which once was meant to serve. He is afraid to miss Mass no matter how barnacled it seems, afraid to marry again no matter how urgent his need, afraid to be himself, afraid to ask what he wants from the Church, afraid to stand alone. A collar can frighten him, a threat from the sanctuary can turn him back, a parent's tears can tear apart his soul. I am not such a Catholic, but I must fight for him, that together we can know the freedom that is God.

This very evening, even as I write, I remember the fortyish man who rang my office bell one summer night. He was tall and lean, athletic and well-dressed, the father of four children, and an usher in our church. His face was sad on this occasion as we settled down solemnly to talk. He told me he was leaving the Church and wanted me to know. He said it wasn't anything personal and that he had grown to consider me his friend. But he was tired of a Church that would not treat him as a man. He was tired of money drives and overcrowded schools, tired of living in a world that only spoke of varieties of sin, tired of empty confessions and rites grown meaningless and cold. He said he was taking his children from our school, where they studied law when he wanted them to learn of love. He wanted them to escape the fears that depressed his wife and him, to learn of God in words that told them they were loved, to grow in confidence and tolerance, to enjoy the world and treat it as a home.

I could not answer him; my defensive eloquence was gone. He was not a complainer, not a wild neurotic, not a proud and angry rebel in the crowd. He was the kind of man I hoped to serve, the kind of man I longed to be, a strong and loyal friend. He shook my hand and thanked me for the services I gave. I asked him why we failed, what he wanted from his Church. He said quietly that all he wanted was a home, a touch of wisdom to see him through the week, a word of mercy that made it all worthwhile, an understanding Church that reminded him of God. Tonight I know why we failed and what he wanted—and I'm sure the man who is a Catholic wants the same.

And I must speak for him because I hear his screams, they echo in my work and in my sleep! He says to me:

"You taught me in my infancy of God. You told me of His angels that followed me to school, His martyrs and His virgins who prayed with me at Mass. You filled my mind with stories that brightened my Christmas and made Lent a dramatic struggle in the company of Christ. You held me in the world of the soul, taught me to pray, introduced me to forgiveness and to sin. You brought the bishop to my Church in all his splendor, told me that my pastor was another Christ. You gathered nuns to teach me and fitted them with crosses that stared at me in school. You gave me a rosary and blessed it, enrolled me in my miraculous medal, and fed me with the sacred food to fill my emptiness. You brought me to holy hours, held relics before my eyes, stuffed my imagination with the saints' heroic deeds. You made religion the center of my life, gave me a reason for living, and promised me the peace that comes from God. You chided my weakness, threatened me with hell, urged me to love, and moved me to pray for the souls still suffering in purgatory's flames. I made the nine First Fridays many times, I honored the Sacred Heart, I said my three 'Hail Mary's' before I slept at night. I gave up movies and candy during Lent, I kept the Fridays, used my missal at Mass, guarded my thoughts, avoided occasions of sin, and honored my parents as best I could. All this you taught me and more. You made me a religious child, a bright and happy child—and when I became a man, you left me.

"You would not listen to the words about the world I tried often to speak to you. I tried to tell you that your promises were not enough, that your words and threats deserted me in the midst of other men. You told me to receive the sacraments, to come more often to Mass, to add a rosary to my daily prayers. I planned to tell you that your service was obsolete, but each time I came near, I feared to be honest. And so I remained a cripple and screamed silently for help. I tried to shake you, but you had formed me too deeply in the mysterious world of God. I tried to ignore you, but I knew not how. Your tales of hell had filtered through my soul. I tried to run from you, but I knew not where to go. And so I stay, a cripple, clinging to my youthful hope of discovering my God.

"This, then, is my dilemma, the dilemma of the man who is a Catholic: I cannot remain a religious child, but you will not let me be an adult. And so I remain a lonely, confused, angry, and abandoned creature, who will not accept an idol, and cannot find his God."

4. THE CATHOLIC PARISH

History offers no finer example of monarchy than the normal Catholic parish. It is a society without genuine channels of recourse, a structure fortified against effective complaint. The pastor can run "his" parish as he will as long as his financial records are reasonably sound. He can guard himself against distressing feedback by prudent control of his flock. If complaints do filter through to the bishop, they are returned to the pastor for "handling." The bishop is generally afraid to quarrel with pastors since removing them from their jobs is a troublesome process.[1] The pastor is the strong man of our system and has received the promotions that years of service and important "connections" can create. If he happens to be a monsignor, for whatever reason, and has some reputation for financial prowess, he is beyond the grasp of human hands.[2]

There are no supervisors to evaluate the pastor's work, no "spies" to inspect his sermons or the educational programs he provides. There is no court that can criticize his handling of the liturgy or his public relations. He can visit hospitals when he likes, knock on doors, or refuse to call on his parishioners. He can decide without consultation the hours of confession, the topics and length of his sermons, whether brides shall dress at home or at the Church, who shall be admitted or evicted from the parish school, who shall use the parish gymnasium, whether there shall be alcohol at a parish dance, and for practical purposes, who can be buried from the Church. He can effectively oppose a new parish that will remove revenue from his own. He can decide who his advisers shall be or if he needs them at all. He can compose or edit the Sunday bulletin, determine how much to pay for a new Church and how soon the parishioners will pay it off. He can hire lay teachers or fire the coach. He can install a new public-address system or remove it and tell his assistant to shout without it. He can hire an organist or forbid music in the Church. He can snarl at people who leave Mass early and refuse to baptize babies whose parents were not married in Church. He can talk money until the people wonder if religion means anything but gold, and he can request an extra collection for any cause he wants. He can have an income that provides him with comforts that none of his people know. He can even ignore Vatican II in loyalty to Trent. There is hardly a parallel for this ecclesiastical phenomenon in all of democratic society, unless it be the bishop he represents. Both cases are simply a matter of frustration without representation.

This is not to say that every Catholic pastor is arrogant and despotic, rather that many are, and that no human being can handle such power. Power can make any man mad. When the man involved has no wife or family, no balanced perception of life's realities, when he functions without criticism or honest advisers, there are almost no limits to the level of his madness.

Historians trace the origins of pastoral authority back to the medieval struggles between the secular or diocesan priests and the monks or religious.[3] In those dark times, secular priests, often without education, were threatened by the growing popularity of the more sophisticated monks, who were not bound to any single parish. These monks could preach to the faithful and accept their offerings despite the protests of the parish priests, because lines of authority were confused. In order to survive, the parish and its pastor were made the legally pampered fortress of the Church. Canon law contains the history of this parochial defense in the decrees which decide where the flock shall pray, where the young shall marry and the old be buried, and especially where the people shall pay.[4] The defense of the parish has lasted to our own day, but with no corresponding protection for the monks. This is why, destined to earn financial support by their imagination, they run their tiny private schools and send us medals and statues through the mail. They are hardly to be blamed for bombarding us with the holy gimmicks when the Church has permitted the parish priest to become its chosen son, with his weekly revenue.

Nothing has changed in five centuries to alter the image of a medieval baron the pastor embodies. Canon law installs him in his parish with stiff dignity. His time off is guaranteed by precise legislation, his rights are those of a Jewish patriarch, and the only responsibility on which he is seriously checked— barring public scandal—is the financial solvency of his parish.

The Catholic pastor, of course, is more than a collection of such medieval laws and canonical protections, history having added a few colors to his coat without asking permission. In addition to his legal status, he is the accumulated compound of a fighter for the immigrants, a scholar to the ignorant, and the proud son of every family. Generations of children have learned never to question his decisions or advice. Young priests who serve under him soon learn how lasting must be their childhood.[5] The pastor is supreme—guarded by law, fortified by history, and defended by his people.

Here and there, indeed, there is some evidence of change. But the dozens of parishes that I have observed closely in the last two years indicate that most of the changes are token and without significance. Pastors are protesting Vatican II even as the people are waiting impatiently for Vatican III. The bishops may have learned at Vatican II that they share the authority of the Pope,[6] but the pastors have failed to learn that they share their power with the people. Catholic people are still dumb and patient sheep, who tip their hat to "Father" and refuse to challenge his arrogance, even as religion loses meaning in their life.

Pastors still urge tithing programs on their pitiful people, and the parish permits fund-raisers to preach the dishonest theology which demands a holy percent. The people fall for the propaganda in the glossy brochures and accept the method of financial contribution which made sense in a religiously ruled society. But a tithing campaign in a world of taxes and government support is a vicious and deceitful gimmick. It hides the needs of nervous pastors to build financial monuments and succeeds under the glib, smooth talk of professional advertisers. Parish after parish promises to tithe under the pressure of a pastor who, while asserting that tithing is the will of God, is not required to justify the costly Church or the obsolete school he builds.

So I watched the silent people tithed, schooled as they are in the docility of non-protest. I do not see the pastors tithed from their vast and unlisted incomes, nor the bishops. Only the people do—piling up money which will be used without their approval, too kind to suspect that often their money merely satisfies their pastor's need to build his kingdom or guarantees his rise toward priestly eminence. But bishops reward pastors whose buildings are expensive and quickly out of debt. Parish holdings are listed in the bishop's name, and faltering mortgages do not show up well on his coat of arms. So the pastor orders the ushers to pass out leaflets at all Masses, preaches each sermon in an important tithing campaign, plugs it as a new insight of modern theology, welcomes the professional fund-raisers from New York and Babylon, and another parish is successfully duped. The people question the fund-raisers in their homes, they express their disgust with them as they ride the bus to work. They wonder why the Church has adopted this impersonal policy in the last few years. But the pastor has spoken, and the gentle sheep will bleat and wag their tails in resigned agreement.

Catholic people do not count. Otherwise, they wouldn't be obliged to listen to the sick sermons they hear. It is a rare Catholic pastor who prepares his sermons; but then, there is no reward from the bishop's office for good preaching. Priests in general are among the poorest speakers in the world. The people continue to come because the fear of mortal sin pressures them, even though the greatest "sin" of all is the priest in his abominable preaching.[7] The dull phrases and stale ideas engraved since childhood, the archaic vocabulary born of Latin theology, the presentation of an idea without feeling or imagination, or what is worse, the presentation of a dull idea with feeling, the abuse of Scripture, the rehashing of personal obsessions—all of this is supposed to prepare the people for the banquet of Christ. Any other organization would go out of business, but the brainwash learned in childhood and the fear of death keeps the pews crowded and the parking lots full.

A decade ago we could, perhaps, endure the impoverished preaching in the Church. Then, at least, the sermon was the only English island in a raging sea of Latin. Then, too, we were wrapped more carefully in our parochial ghetto. We were taught to carry home whatever little defective pearl was offered and to overlook the irrelevance that proved we had been to Mass. We did not then know that the sermon was to be the incisive word that Christ spoke to us at the common meal to interpret life to His brothers.[8] It was rather a defense of the system, a reminder of the details of the catechism forgotten since grade school, or commercial time to plug money or the sacraments, or to attack birth control and steady dating. The pastor was in charge and we accepted what he condescended to give.

And we do it still. We hear the long harangues on parish finances or listen to the dull letters explaining diocesan collections. We hear missionaries tell snake and lion stories to solicit more money. Last week I heard a pastor read all of the Mass intentions for the week even though they were listed in the bulletin. He then announced three meetings and gave the details of the next fiscal campaign. He bawled out the mothers for letting their daughters wear shorts and slacks downtown and told the adults that they were far too interested in pleasure and money. He proved this by stating that only one out of three envelopes had been used by contributors the previous week. Then he told us to say "Ay-men" and not "Ah-men" at communion time, and to place our hands on the table when we received. We were also to lean forward as long as we were not wearing low-cut gowns. After this "sermon" he returned to the altar and no one in the Church shook a fist or threw a brick. Ten years ago I would have admired the flock's restraint. Now I found myself lamenting their ignorance. They did not know what the sermon was supposed to mean. Luther had told them four hundred years ago about the importance and meaning of the sermon, but Luther has never sold too well in Catholic pamphlet racks.[9] The pastor had spoken and the patient adults and their squirming children listened.

But some did not listen. They had the good sense to remain away, or to seek out a pastor who makes an attempt to communicate. These are the people who cannot bear to hear words about God and man which only make them angry and bored. They cannot submit to a half hour of pious irrelevance that keeps them twitching in their seats. They do not ask much, and if they find a priest who preaches fairly well, he becomes a Fulton Sheen in present competition. They may even search in vain for such a priest, because there are no bonuses for preaching.

They walk away in ever greater numbers, but they do not walk away with uncomplicated ease. The aura of the Mass lingers in the memories carried from childhood, and they look in vain for substitutes. It is generally not the old who leave, since they are closer to eternity and have learned patience in the face of life's inanities. It is the young, because they demand more of life and still hope to find answers for the questions that will not be quiet. Thus far it seems that they are not missed, since the Churches are still full, the collections still fat. The pastors can continue to preach without preparation, and the people accept their religious "home" without right of protest.

It would be naïve simply to blame pastors or bishops for the lack of intelligent sermons, though such blame would not be totally without truth. I am blaming, rather, a parochial

system that permits a pastor to run his parish without the
reaction and suffrage of his flock. I am blaming a training
program that does not insist on the importance of preaching
in God's work. Years are spent in mastering theology which
can be learned in months, and minutes are given to preaching
which should have required hours. The Sunday sermon is the
single most important avenue of communication that a priest
has. No business can assemble all of its customers at once.
Few leaders have fifteen precious and guarded minutes in
which to address their people. But the priest does have this
rare opportunity and he readies himself by jotting down a few
notes during TV commercials or he "thinks it out" on his feet.
He cannot preach because he does not have to, and the system
which protects the pastor from the rage of his people is decadent and out of date.

Good preaching and an intelligible liturgy are necessary for
the Church's survival in an age of discordant noises. The world
in which we could simply remind man of his obligations and
expect conformity is giving way to a world that wants relevance and communication. Once we could point to the mystery of the Mass and sacraments, and wait for man to come
for his portion of grace. Now we know that there must be
words to render the Mass and sacraments meaningful.[10] Man
will not be satisfied with the silent forms that do not tell him
of the mystery they contain, for this is to be satisfied with a
silent Christ.

I hoped, for a time, that songs and English in the Mass
would solve the problem of our bored and indifferent people.
I thought that the obvious failure of our liturgical renewal was
due to the resistance of the untouchable pastors. And yet, as
the pastors have accepted the untrained laymen in the sanctuaries and scattered song sheets in the pews, I realize just how
pitiable is our preaching. The liturgy is bad enough with its
experimental confusion and its disorganized motion, which
cannot compete with the meditative silence of the past. A
liturgical reform, however, understandably takes time. But
there is no excuse for our horrid preaching, and yet it does

not seem to change. The bright young men with their new theology are as dull and pointless as their pastors; if anything, a trifle duller and less convincing.

Recently I made a survey of the sermons in thirty different parishes in five separate states, listening to an average of four sermons in each parish. The results of my study—however modest—are appalling. Only two of more than a hundred sermons I heard were worthy of an average audience. Money was mentioned with lengthy enthusiasm more than 40 percent of the time. In at least twelve of the parishes it is customary to read long excerpts from the bulletin. In at least ten of the parishes the public-address system is inadequate. Frequently I was scolded, even insulted, and most of the time I was talked down to. When the new laws came out on mixed marriages, lifting the censure of excommunication from those married outside the Church, I only heard that this did not mean that these invalidly married sinners were free from mortal sin. I heard nothing of the hope that this new legislation might contain, or the possibility of a more tolerant view of mixed marriage in the future. I was only told that the offenders were "living in sin" and could not be expected to be "buried from the Church."

But we hardly need private or public studies. We have simply to permit laymen to speak with unguarded honesty. Speak to them of the sermons they hear and ask them if they leave Church with a message that gives practical meaning to the realities of life. They will tell you of sermons which give evidence that "Father" has spent twice as much time with the Sunday paper as he has with sermon preparation.

Maybe every priest should not attempt to preach, certainly some should not. Priests without financial ability are quietly sent to parishes where they can do no harm. But wretched preachers, as long as they can raise money, are promoted to an even larger flock. Within the last few years, I served in a prominent parish—one with a number of sophisticated people —where the pastor spends every other Sunday lecturing his flock about their tardiness at Mass. The pastor is firmly founded in his parish, since he has efficiently handled an important administrative post in the diocese. His preaching, however, does injustice to fourth-graders. The tardiness of the parishioners could be helped if he gave shorter sermons and enlarged the parking lot. But no one can convince him that anything but selfishness keeps the people coming late.

For months he required the ushers to lock the Church doors once the Mass had begun, even though the Church was located downtown and served the visitors to the city. I admit that he is a neurotic but, after all, there is no avenue of recourse for the parishioners. He screams at the altar boys, barks at the communicants, insults the people regularly from the pulpit. To hear his sermon is to leave the Church a nervous wreck. I grant that he is a bit more colorful than the majority of poor preachers and impossible pastors, but thousands of Catholics can relate similar experiences. A man in any other profession would lose his job, but the Catholic pastor is beyond complaint.

If you want good sermons and intelligent religious leadership, you must demand it from us. Begin by cutting your contribution in half, or by paying for the value you receive. But do not act silently or without explanation. Tell us why you have ceased to pay. There is no other way to reach us in the present structure of the Church. The pastor is a man who does not have to listen until enough people refuse to pay.

Do anything but excuse us, or our irrelevance will grow, and the exodus of the faithful will increase. We can learn to preach, even though our seminary training did not teach us how. We learned to gather money without a course in economics, to run a parish school without a text in education or commerce. We will learn to communicate when the people demand it. We will throw away the tawny sermon books and the outlines in periodicals which have given us printed substitutes for thought. We will preach when we take the time to read and reflect and begin to discard the overworked platitudes that we haven't practiced in years.

Not only do the people have nothing to say about the public relations and sermons in the average parish, but also they are practically boycotted from the parish school. The present policy is to build centralized schools to replace the individual parish schools of the past. Each parish is assessed for a central school or tithed to death to sustain its own. This policy continues even though there is serious question if they accomplish anything except to perpetuate the ghetto and, in some cases, to help the middle-class white keep their children from attending schools with Negroes. We will discuss the problem of parochial schools in another chapter, but here we merely point out that a parish can pour thousands of dollars into Catholic education without the consent of the parishioners. A pastor, sent to America as a missionary from Ireland, can and frequently does impose his rural views of education on an American parish. No matter that his intelligent parishioners teach in public schools or lecture at state universities. They are forced to hear the praises of an educational system which is hard pressed to justify its existence. They may sincerely believe that religious education comes largely, if not exclusively, from the home, and yet they are "forced" to support the parochial school of the local parish. For years we have complained through our "official" episcopal spokesman that we have been taxed to support schools we didn't use. No one seems to notice that every Catholic parish is guilty of a similar violation.

Nor do the people have anything to say about the liturgical reforms that rock the parishes with clumsy force. A few years back the people were required to recite prayers in gibberish Latin which they didn't understand. Then they were told to sing hymns, to listen to a variety of untrained laymen, and to abandon ancient liturgy without anything comparable to take its place. There was more than a grain of truth in the wisdom of Father DePauw's insistence that the traditional Catholics had been ignored.[11] It would seem more accurate to say that the Catholic people have been "traditionally ignored" in every major decision which affected their personal lives. They have been forced, and still are, to adopt a series of liturgical symbols that are meaningful only in the innocent lives of a group of esoteric Church historians who call themselves "liturgists." To reform the liturgy demands a knowledge of men. Simply to permit the president of the altar society to carry the cruets to the altar or to erect communion stations or Bible stands in the sanctuary means little or nothing to the men I know. We need a sense of community, and the latest dreams of the liturgical in-group won't provide us with anything more than another golden calf. The people, meanwhile, have nothing to say, and they wait for the next "inane" suggestion from the desk of some doting cardinal.

There will be a parish someday in which the people will have an honest voice, and it had better be soon.[12] There will be a parish which will have to concern itself with modern novelties such as public relations and the art of communication. In order to bring this about, both the collection and expenditure of money will have to be in hands other than the pastor's, because no man can sensibly handle his vast power without the present abuse. It will be the people's parish and they will support it willingly when they have a voice in its administration and the quality of its service! Parishes will have to be much smaller so as to foster a sense of community somewhere besides in the heads of all-knowing liturgists. No community can exist without dialogue and a practical share in some obvious work, and no amount of liturgical reforms or prayer cards will alter that fact.

The parish of the future will admit a married clergy. To think otherwise is to be hopelessly ignorant. This will provide the priests that are needed, something which no amount of nagging or vocational "pitchmen" will accomplish. The priesthood is still attractive to a large number of young men, but it will not continue so if the priest is not free to choose or to sacrifice marriage. With an adequate number of priests, the Church can go to people and not expect man to adapt his needs to the worn-out structures of the Church. Some people may well be satisfied with a large parish, since they derive a sense of community in the impersonal Churches of the metropolis. For most men, however, there can be no community in a parish of five or ten thousand people. A subway station at the rush hour is as personal and intimate. The priest will have to know his people,[13] and this will be at least possible in a Church of five hundred souls. He can employ a layman to help him with the parish books and finances, and not depend on the obsolete commodity of volunteer help.

In such a parish he will not have to build a school, since his knowledge of his people and a couple of trained nuns could provide him with all the staff he needs. Nor will he wait until he is fifty or sixty to be a pastor. He could well be ready to accept a parish at ordination if his seminary education would abandon the "myth" of preparing "theologians" and begin to educate men of faith to preach, counsel, and think. He will not spend twenty or thirty years as the assistant to an omnipotent pastor, and lose his fire and ideals in the process. He will even have the freedom to make mistakes, and contact with a parish council will provide him with greater direction than any diocesan office could ever give. He will, of course, be paid a reasonable salary, and not be forced to rely on clever financial "angles" and mounds of "unreported income." This would put an end to the scandal of "Mass stipends" and seat collections, and a dozen other ecclesiastical games. He could even return the Christmas and Easter donations of the struggling pensioners which keep him from starvation in the Hiltons both here and abroad.

Nor will the priest of the future be strapped with the obsolete organizations that cripple the work of the priest in the parish. He will not need a St. Vincent de Paul Society to help the poor if he encourages his parishioners to investigate the channels of social welfare and to improve them. Nor will he spend his time with a Holy Name Society, which flounders around searching for some modern apostolate. He can abandon the Athletic Association when he permits the children of his flock to take advantage of the programs which satisfy the other children of the community. He can even disband the Altar Society, which spends each fall pleading for members and each spring wondering what in the world to do with them. He won't even need the Legion of Mary, whose archaic name is symbolic of its archaic program. It would, of course, mean an end to that historic cornerstone called bingo, unless it were salvaged to occupy our neglected senior citizens. He won't even have to build a convent, since the sisters can live in a neighborhood like everyone else and know the freedom that maturity and responsibility require.

The rescinding of the Friday law of abstinence permits us to hope that soon enough Sunday Mass will not be an obligation. Even now I question emphatically that missing Mass can bind under pain of "mortal sin." Mass will not have to "oblige" in a small community which cares about the people and teaches them to care about one another. Nor will there be a daily Mass in the Church to satisfy the sisters and the janitor. The priest will offer Mass in homes, or factories, or shopping centers, and its form will be brief and casual enough to admit restless children and holy enough to remind man of God. There will be no need of processions and gadgets to tell people they are a community. There will be a liturgy that flows from a genuine community, and not one that presumes or forces it. The freedom for variety and experiment will rest with local groups and not follow national directives in a nation which includes hundreds of levels. Boundaries will mean nothing next to the common experience which the community shares. The Mass can be as long or short as the community requires. It will be as brief and to the point as modern life, and yet provide the minutes of mystery and reverence that a profane man must have.[14]

It will, of course, be in the people's language, every syllable of it. It will consist of no more than readings from Scripture, an honest word from the priest, prayer, offering, and sacrifice. There will be time for simple ceremony, but none for enervating pomp. There will be time for the people to speak of their sick, their dying, their children, their joys, but none for collections or financial plugs or eloquent verbiage. The community will know each other's names and jobs and children, and will be taught through time and effort to communicate as friends. The people will not find it so hard to be friends, because the priest will be first their friend and only then their high priest.

Groups in the parish will be organized according to parochial needs. Non-Catholics will feel at home in this liturgy without the meaningless barnacles of tradition. The Mass will require no more explanation than a happy family, or a home-cooked meal, or a meaningful conversation. The parish will be a place of service which seeks to make God live among men and to help men discover God in mutual love. Long enough have we talked of community and offered only an auditorium. Song does not bring people together, be they Kiwanians or Catholics. We prove nothing when we pray aloud together; it is only when we live together or work together that common prayer means community.

We need such a parish, a home where man can belong. We need a religious family where a man can know the priest he speaks to, and can tell him of his fears and hopes. We hardly need theology classes for the occasional enthusiast; we need to practice religion. We don't need Catholic welfare programs or Catholic hospitals; we need only to recognize the aims that we have in common with all men. Then the vocabulary of Vatican II, such as "people of God" and "citizens of the kingdom," will not strike us as being as irrelevant as the language which it replaced. Too much of our renewed language is only another barrier to understanding, too many of our symbols speak to no one save the scholars who fashioned them. A parish will be a family only when it acts like one, not when we suggest parallels in complex analogies.

In such a parish we can find the peace and meaning that a ghetto world found in the comfort of its familiar surroundings. When the ghetto world grew, and the children climbed over its walls, there remained only an institution which offered us Mass and the sacraments, even though we called it a Church. Now we recognize how vast and impersonal it has become, and how quickly man runs to find his religious home in other communities that do not smother and swallow him. The lodge, the barbecue, group therapy, the beach, the golf course, the retirement village, the poker club will have to provide all the community that man needs until the parish truly becomes a family of friendship in God. One wonders how long we will have to wait.

5. THE LOSS OF

PERSONALISM

Deep in the heart of a modern city lives a man. He moves in a world of turnpikes and suburbs, owns a dozen suits with a pair of ties for each. Vietnam is as real to him as the taxes that cloud his every spring. Each new wrinkle on his face warns him of the young college graduate who is struggling to supplant him. Another child in his family can mean a new home. A high-school graduation can mean another college tuition. He watches the stock market, worries about retirement, and observes the bulging waistline that can bury him at fifty. He wonders what he has done with his life, wonders why he rushes so, and asks why he and his wife have grown apart. He was raised a Catholic. He seldom misses Mass and keeps Lent with honest concern. He receives communion once a month, has contributed to a half-dozen churches and their building funds. He takes a drink almost every day, about as often as he has indigestion and a nervous stomach. He frequently plans a program of daily exercise. His office is a daily rerun of Space Headquarters when an Agena rocket misfires. He rushes his lunch, fights the traffic on his way from work, and glances through a couple of newspapers. He has heard of the Good Shepherd, the land of many mansions, and the raging fires of hell. He has been told to be kind and forgiving, to control his thoughts, to pray for the dead. He is a Catholic, but his faith seems to miss him at the center of his life.

High in the mountains of Mexico I have often watched the simple Indians practice their faith. A roadside shrine decorates the highway, a burst of fireworks announces a wedding or a first communion. Here in the world of grass huts and corn tortillas, the war in Vietnam does not exist. There is no concern about styles or stock markets. A skinny burro, grazing by the highway, asks only slightly less of life than does his master. Each man seems to know his special task, and the very hardships of his life point to another world where the torrential rains cease and the shoulders do not ache under a load of wood. Juan lives here and is a practical Catholic. He has been taught some simple prayers and says them with great devotion. He attends Mass when there is a priest around to offer it, and finds it the most exciting pageant that a life without TV or transportation provides. The laws he follows are as uncomplicated as his life. He prays to the Madonna, feeds his children, and is kind to his wife. Occasionally he drinks too much. He may snicker at an obscene joke, or cast an unsavory glance at his blossoming daughter. He asks no more of life than its measure of meals and rest, a thatched roof to shield his family from showers, and children to support him when he can no longer stoop to plant the corn. He has heard of the Good Shepherd, the land of many mansions, and the raging fires of hell. He has been told to be kind and forgiving, to control his thoughts, to pray for the dead. He is a Catholic and his faith is as normal and natural as his sheep.

Juan did not choose his world of mountains and grazing goats, nor did the city man ask to live in the orbit of speed and ulcers. They are, indeed, brothers in Christ, locked in a life they cannot completely control. To each of them the Church has been commissioned by Christ to speak, but it cannot hope to reach them with an identical message and approach. Even a generation ago, a univocal system would not have been so difficult. Today it is impossible.

Once I could live in the religious world of Juan with only

slight nuances of distinction. It was the world of my parents and the ghetto I have already mentioned.

Our sincerity as Catholics was as much the result of nationalism as of simple and superstitious faith. To be Irish, or Polish, or Italian was to be Catholic, and the brogues and accents were as slow to disappear as the uncompromising fury of our faith. To have a priest of one's own nationality was more important than having a priest. To commemorate the customs and folkways of Europe was as religious as to observe the rubrics of the Mass. Parish suppers were more the mark of the Catholic community than the congregation that knelt each Sunday in the parish Church. And the courage that led us regularly to sacrifice and prayer was fed as much by antipathies born in Europe as by faith born of God. Behind our minority courage was a starving theology which supported closed minds and encouraged unrelenting law.

Even the Protestant world, with all its historic freedom, strangled under the grasp of an idealism which was as sure Rome was wrong as Catholics were that it was right. The political speeches of that day rang with the positive assurance that man would solve the social problem. Education, too, was sure of its goal and confident of its methods. The curriculum was settled and enshrined, and teachers seemed to know the courses and disciplinary devices that could mold a man. Even science, though its methods promised a never-ending search for truth, was pompous in its certitudes and arrogant in its facile promises. In such a world, the world of Juan and my parents, the world of my youth, my Church could easily survive. But in today's world, the world of the city man, little is certain, little—if anything—can be codified.

I did not choose my world. I merely live in it and struggle to remain a person in loyalty to the uniqueness handed me by God.[1] I cannot think as every other Catholic, nor can I have a conscience that accepts the charted program which suits another man. I do not require specific laws which bind my fingers and chain my feet. True, such laws may restrain me from striking my neighbor or stomping his children, but they also bar me from learning how to love. I need general directions, not detailed rules. I need confidence and motivation, not anxiety and orders. I have outgrown the mother who tells me when to eat, and when to sleep, and how to know a flower from a weed. I am a person, not a cardboard man, a man in search, and not a sheltered child. No church can change me, I must change myself. No code can regulate my soul, no creed can satisfy my thirst.

Creeds can only be offered, but *I* must take them to myself.[2] No one can tell me that I *must* embrace each shred of mystery, each symbol of the Trinity, each glory of Mary, each theory of death and judgment, each exaggerated dogma on the divinity of Christ, if I am to be a member of my Church. You can only explain to me your faith, reveal to me the tiny light you find in darkness, expose to me what gives you hope and warms your love, and know that God and I will do the rest. I am a *person*, free and struggling, living in light and darkness, walking the edge of love and hate, hope and despair, openness and narrowness, fear and courage. God is closer to me than my Church, closer than doctrine and ritual, closer than sacrament or saint. My Church can only be my servant, not my parent. It can only offer me truth, not cram it down my throat. It can only speak of God, not reduce Him to a cautious list of words.

Nor can a code contain His total will.[3] No woman can blueprint for a man each motion of his love, unless she wants a slave. She cannot direct his words, regulate his feelings, outline his duties, enforce his steps. She can only offer her love, reveal her feelings, suggest her hurts, whisper her fears, engage his attention, describe her needs, and hope that he will respond. A Church can do no more unless it plans to desecrate the persons it was commissioned to serve. It is no servant of Christ if it is satisfied with an ignorant people too docile to be persons. What does it gain if it wins compliance at the cost of personal love? Fear is not love, nor is listless silence.

Can I not kneel with my brothers if I do not share each facet of their faith? How will faith grow if I cannot compare the feebleness of mine with the strength of theirs? Can I not eat with my brothers at a common table unless I comply with laws that are as senseless to me as they are helpful to them? Are faith and love a single thing, a category, a catechism definition, the vision of a medieval mind? No man can tell me he believes, but only that he is poised between faith and doubt, certitude and despair. Faith is not a static thing, it is as dynamic and nebulous as life. No man possesses faith, or embraces it; he only grows a trifle farther from his unbelief. He can only struggle like the blind man in the Gospel and beg humbly, "Help thou my unbelief."

Faith is the jungle path that leads a man to see a glimmer of his God, not the well-marked superhighway that takes him from the earth. It is a beginning, a spark, not a clear and comprehensive summary of God. Must I believe as you do to have it? Must I say "I believe" to satisfy my Church when I can only say with honesty "I try"? Do you want a particular word from me, a meaningless assent? Then you forbid me to be a person in my life within my Church. Do I believe in the Trinity? I am not sure. I can say I do and tell you how long I tried to ponder it. I am not opposed to it, but it does not seem to reach me in my heart. God reaches me, so does Jesus, but I cannot keep their persons straight. Nor can I make an important friend of person number three. Do I believe in purgatory? I do not know. I only know that such a dogma does not cause me concern. Nor do indulgences, or angels, or devils, or special devotions to Mary and the saints.

I have a similar difficulty with morals and with law. I see couples remarry after divorce and I inwardly approve. Must I say that I don't to be a member of my Church? Again, you ask me to deny that I am a person, to ignore the experience that speaks to me of God. It is the same with birth control, or Sunday Mass, or sterilization, or mixed marriage: must I view them as every other Catholic to have a home within the Church? If so, I am asked to prostitute my person to enjoy the service of my Church. This I cannot do.

Man is more important than a system, and older than the

Church. The Church is for me and I cannot be silent when it ignores the personalism that Christ purchased with His blood. It has forgotten me and the other weak men. It counts me as one of its statistics and rejects me as a son. It demands I recite its dogmas and commands and that I accept its laws. It speaks to me in rites and symbols I barely understand. Its priests preach to me and I cannot answer back. Its ceremonies bore me and I cannot effect a change. I am forced to attend a Mass that has lost touch with the world in which I live. I sit and hear a sermon which makes me struggle to keep my faith. I listen to the ritual changes sent from Rome and I wonder if the men who made them have enough passion to sin, enough fire to hate, enough life to love.

I enter the confessional as a penitent and I am dispatched as a nameless face. My struggles do not matter, my agony counts for naught. I hear confessions as a priest and I am forbidden to understand. A bachelor tries to describe his first honest relationship with a woman and I shout at him of sex. I want to encourage him, to nourish his love, to strengthen his confidence, to praise him for the promiscuity he has abandoned, and I hear myself saying, "Marry her, or give it up." I hear his feeble protest and sense his fear. He tries to speak and I smother him with words. He grows angry and so do I. He came for love, for help, for Christ, and received a formula, an impersonal rebuff. I am forbidden to be a person in my Church, and the men who come to me for mercy and light are denied the same unique and Godlike right.

Voices spoke out long ago insisting that the Church was forbidding Catholics the chance to be persons in the Church. John Henry Newman (1801–1890), the great English scholar, recognized the Church's futility in forcing a system on man, refusing him the chance to search for a personal faith. Newman insisted that it was wrong to forbid a man the chance to seek within the framework of the Church when seeking was the very condition of true faith. The Church forbade a man to entertain doubts, and forbids it still, and attempted to enforce a body of propositions with an assemblage of logical supports that were logical only to the man who believed. Newman sensed our irrelevance when he said: "Logic makes but sorry rhetoric with the multitude; first shoot around corners, and you may not despair of converting by a syllogism. . . . To most men argument makes the point in hand only more doubtful and considerably less impressive."[4]

Newman understood—as did Max Scheler of Germany (d. 1929) and Maurice Blondel of France (d. 1949),[5] religious philosophers who criticized their Church—that religious experience is a personal communication between man and his God. God exists only when He becomes my God, and not merely when I can support Him with my arguments. Religion cannot be imposed from without. A nineteenth-century French scholar wrote that religious truth is: "A person who gives up his secret only to one who is deserving, not as something knowable from without."[6] Or, as Blondel, a layman, wrote at the turn of our century: "[Faith] is not a question of a theoretical adherence to a dogma which is external to us, but the practical insertion into our hearts and conduct of a lifegiving truth."[7] These were the voices of personalism, voices which recalled a Christianity long since dead. Such voices were called dangerous and their thoughts have not until recently come to life within my Church. They were largely lumped with a group called "Modernists," who were condemned by Pope Pius X at the turn of our century.

It is unfortunate that the Church condemned them in such a universal and defensive way. The Modernists understood the needs of modern man. They had seen religion grow stale and impersonal, and in the midst of their exaggerations they clung to an all-important truth: Religion had to find a response within the heart of man. It could not be imposed from without by fear, and long remain relevant. A religion of duty and obligation could only produce pharisees and children. It could make national boundaries more important than God and support the armies of France and Germany, which killed each other in the name of peace. The Church condemned the Modernists because they made God into a creature of man. But at least the Modernists recognized that the Christian Churches had turned God into a system of dogma without devotion, duty without warmth, and law without love. My Church had become a frightened old lady saying her rosary and dreaming of hell. My Church was impersonal and the Modernists were honest enough to admit it, honest enough to be condemned.[8]

Modernism, however, did not die, it only matured. It has clarified its position and demanded that religion be not a docile allegiance to a body of propositions, but an honest search for meaning and for truth. The Church has never given Modernists a chance, and even now, a half century after Pius X's condemnation of the Modernist "heresy," each new priest is asked to swear an oath against it. It is like asking Americans to deny their loyalty to a British King. But young priests swear the oath. Some laugh about it, but some are still too trapped even to laugh. They recite solemnly its mossy paragraphs and promise to preserve the Church from the sinister invasions of modern thought. The hierarchy should rather demand that each priest read the pages of the Modernists rather than condemn them in boyish ignorance. The Modernists were as alive as we are dead. They could distinguish a man from a clinging shadow and knew that religious faith was sick. The "God is dead" prophets are only the wordy children that the Modernists have spawned because no one took them seriously. They demanded that the Church permit a man to be a person, and fifty years later I must still demand.

There must be a place for persons in the Church, a place for differences, a place for variety of search.[9] Is there no place in the Church for the man who only begins to believe? Are there not presently, despite our condemnations and courageous front, as many kinds of Catholics within the Church itself as there are divisions of Protestants and Jews? I am closer to the faith of many ministers than to that of many fellow priests. I know rabbis who are more Christian than I, and unbelievers with whom I share a religious closeness I seldom find at home. Does this mean that I am not a Catholic? Or does it mean that I am beginning to be a person in my Church?

That I *must* be a person seems so simple and obvious it is difficult to determine how my Church has strayed. Somehow in the world of emperors and kings my Church became arrogant, and it perverted the authority handed it by Christ. It forgot the image of the Shepherd and mimicked all the panoply of kings. The king, surrounded with lords, was supreme. He could be benevolent or cruel, tolerant or calloused, but his decisions were absolute and beyond all recourse. It was a simple world, a decisive world, and it became the only world that could mold the Catholic Church. It taught the Pope to call himself a shepherd while men carried him on a throne. It gave the bishops rings to extend to docile lips, and filled our sanctuaries with incense and brocade. A modern man, removed from such traditions by time, painfully senses the discordant horror of this incredible display. His President wears a business suit, eats hot dogs, and shakes the people's hands. Modern man can play golf with his boss or share a beer with him in a backyard barbeque. He calls his doctor "Bill," and his banker "Bob," and drives on highways where deference is almost indecent. He is not unaware of the symbols of power and prestige, but he has learned that only the mightily insecure must support their office with pomp and silk. He wonders at a Pope who eats alone like an unfriendly mystic or retires to a summer castle to solve the birth-control problem for the world. Modern man wants to be a person and he cannot fathom this childish world of cabbages and kings.

It would be intolerable enough if our priests and bishops saw themselves as governors and corporation presidents, which they very often do. It makes me sad enough when I cannot see a shepherd but only a businessman, or I see only a shepherd who treats me like a sheep. But when I must bow my head before their majesty and hold my tongue no matter what they do, I know that my Church has sold its birthright for the scepter of a king. And a great body of thought, the decadent theology of the Catholic Church, has told her she is right. Catholic theology, which died somewhere between Thomas and Tarzan, permits the Pope to be as untouchable as an emperor, the bishop to be an independent lord, and even the pastor to rule without regard for the person that is man. Until Catholic theology ceases to be an archaic defense of obsolete forms, there cannot be persons in the Church.[10] There can be only quiet serfs who await the orders of a king. There can be no protests, no revolutions, no genuine reforms. The years of Vatican II will remain a superficial gesture by a frightened Church, until theology discovers it is dead.

What has Vatican II really done to make us persons? Has it really helped us by permitting our Mass in English when the prayers and ceremonies continue to leave us cold? Are we persons now that the bishops have voted to share the medieval powers of our Pope? Or do we only have a greater distribution of the same unyielding game? Are we persons now that we have finally freed the Jews and Protestants from our arrogance and wrath? Or have we only duped them into lesser anger when their children marry in our parish Church? Are we persons now that we have promised to respect the religious conscience of each man? Or have we only mumbled words whose meaning still escapes?

Ask the Catholic man whose wife had three affairs before he threw her out. Ask him if his conscience is free. Ask him if Vatican II gave him the permission to marry again, to replace a baby sitter with a wife, to make the decision he's made each night a thousand times. Ask the widow who fears another marriage, but cannot promise to live without the beauty of love and sex. Ask her if the bishops, gathered in august council, solved anyone's problems but their own. Ask the college graduate who hears the normal sermons in his Church and wonders if hell's loneliness could ever be as bad. Ask him if he is a person in his Church, and if the recent council fortified his faith.

Nothing has really changed. We are still as helpless and frightened as before. We will still stand back and watch the humanist struggle with the problems of man. We will continue to preserve the system that has paralyzed us and only offer reforms that are dull and out of date. The authority that forbids us to be persons remains untouchable. The theology that protects this authority is afraid to face itself. Biology did not die with Linnaeus or Lamarck, nor did medicine grow rigid with Harvey and Pasteur. But Catholic theology is a barely stirring corpse, too weak and frightened to leave the universities, too superficial to strike at roots, too timid to move among simple and honest men.

But honest men are not satisfied. They are raging and the world has just begun to hear their cry. They long to be persons more than they have been permitted to realize. Their personalism is not of yesterday. It looks back a hundred years. It is in their blood, in their culture, in the angry silence of their heart. Each decade the vision has grown a little clearer, each decade courageous voices have gained a little strength. Newman did not speak in vain from England, nor did the French priest Lammenais, who died without the Church. They are long dead, as are Blondel and Reusselot, who fought the Church's arrogance in France. Chardin is gone, and so is Buber, and Tillich, too, can speak no more. The simple man has never read them and might not even recognize their names. No matter! He has heard them in the ball parks and the barbershops, in the taverns and restaurants, in simple words, without deference to the author or the text. He has heard them and my Church will know his rage.

He will demand that the Church permit him to be a person, that it serve and not absorb him in his search for God. The Church has no choice. It will hear him, satisfy him, or become a museum for the timid and helpless few. Blondel, the French philosopher, wrote fifty years ago:

There are two ways of looking at the history of philosophical ideas. Either we remain outside the main stream which sweeps through the world of thought and radically exclude everything which is opposed to the system we have adopted . . . and that is to cut ourselves off . . . Or else we try to perceive the birth pangs of humanity and profit by this vast effort, to enlighten it, to bring it to fruition.[11]

Man will not long listen to a Church that ignores the person in a world that has changed superstition into science. My Church is not a big thing in Europe and struggles for its very life. Even in conservative America, the children of the immigrants have learned to read. The protests grow stronger and the smiling peasants start to frown. Man has listened long enough to the severe condemnations of birth control and steady dating, to financial plans which cater to suburban comfort and create schools of questionable value, when overpopulation, war, and the brutality of an industrialized society threaten the humanity he has. Man searches for direction and identity, and hears dull, doctrinal sermons which presume a loyalty that was never asked. He looks for a key to life in a world of pressure and speed, and he is scolded for his failure to receive the sacraments or tithe or support the men's club. Once he could be held by the pressure of his family or the threat of excommunication or the fear of hell. Now, however, if the Church does not reach him, respect him, hear him, he will search for God in his own way. Only a servant Church can assist him in his quest of self and God. He must be a person, because he was made a man.

6. THE CHURCH OF THE LEGAL CODE

I had spent three months giving Doug instructions in the Catholic faith, and I could see that he pondered my words seriously. One night he told me that he wanted to join my Church and to marry Martha, the Catholic girl who sat with him during each conference. I liked Doug. He was twenty-eight, tall and intense, and three months from his degree in engineering. A place called Korea had postponed his education, a girl called Martha had given direction to his life. I heard him describe in simple language what the Christian vision meant to him. I saw Martha study his lips as he talked.

He told me that his parents had seldom gone to Church. He called himself a Methodist, but knew nothing of the simplicity and beauty of that faith. He had learned a few prayers, knew by heart a handful of scriptural texts, but abandoned all religion in the thrill of high school "sophistication" and sex. Once, he admitted, he had thought that financial success would quiet the rage of his heart. He had been ruthless in his ambition, cynical in his vision of the world. He had smothered the secret protests of his soul with drink and endless activity.

Religion had scarcely occurred to him again until he spent a couple of lonely and frightened nights on one of Korea's hills in the company of a young chaplain. Doug liked this man, and learned from him that God could be found in the warmth of friendship or in the struggle to draw meaning from the insanity of life. He experienced the same longing for God in his love of Martha and could not be truly close to her until he shared her simple faith. He said, with obvious embarrassment, that he had never known that life could be so alive. His words did not come easily, the pauses were punctuated by the agitation of his face. It was beautiful to see and hear, to know that I had helped him in his search for God.

I looked at Martha and saw the eyes of youthful love. She was twenty-four, a graduate of a Catholic college, a petite beauty who had asked me to give religious instructions to her man. She had dated a dozen others, traveled to Europe, held a challenging job, and won the affection of many friends. Now she had found the man who would not let her mind be quiet until she pledged to him her body and her heart. She was one of the joys of my priesthood, one of the complex creatures who had penetrated my defenses and involved me in her life. Her silence was eloquent and I could feel the force of her love.

Then, quietly, Doug told me that there was something else I should know. He had been married before at eighteen and lived with his bride for eleven months. He said that it had really been no marriage at all, rather, the result of a young man's fears when he discovered that his steady girl was pregnant. They had been married quietly in the Methodist Church to appease her parents and the chagrin of his righteous father. Doug had fought with her, slapped her, wept and slept with her. But he didn't love her, and actually felt relieved when she lost the baby at seven months. He wanted out, but his father insisted that he live up to his vow. He tried a few months more, to no avail, and by mutual agreement he and his teenage bride were divorced. Then it was service, school, and Martha.

He looked for my reaction and waited for my words. I was confused; the proper legal questions were biting at my lips. I knew that if he and his first "bride" had been baptized in their faith, there was nothing left for anyone to do. But I had to ask the questions. I learned that Doug had been baptized at the age of twelve to please his father's mother, even though he and his father never went to Church. His bride, too, had been christened in her faith and was as ignorant of its meaning as he. But both had been baptized, exchanged "consent," and had marital intercourse, and this would make their marriage forever binding in the awesome courts of Rome.

Doug could beg for consideration because of youthful fear and parental force, and Rome might theoretically accept his excuse. But it could not be proved, and Roman lawyers only want the facts. My submitting his case would be tragically in vain. Doug had no case, only an honest story and a human heart, which would count for naught in the laws and canons of my Church. He could say that baptism had meant nothing to him, that he had not understood the meaning of a married love in Christ. That would not matter. Rome would only want to know if the water of baptism had flowed on his skin, if he had agreed to the marriage, if he had slept in fleshly union with his wife.

I was upset, but my mind continued to struggle with the law. Could I lie for Doug when I knew that he had every right to take Martha as his wife? I did not have the courage. Could I ignore his first marriage? No, the calls would come from the angry and wounded "sinners" who had been denied a marriage in my Church. Could I plead with the bishop, the Pope? No, I would be treated with disdain and would be asked to re-examine the clear and simple law. There was nothing I could do. Doug and his teen-age bride were locked in an eternal union by the canonists of Rome. Doug and his gentle Martha were destined to frustration and defeat. I was trapped, and so were they, regardless of the decision our personal consciences made.

Doug stared at me in unbelief as he read the answer in my eyes. He asked me "Why?" and heard my stupid answer with patient grief. He protested that he had never known what marriage meant, that the pregnancy had scared him half to death. I felt the knot in my stomach as I spoke, the knot that was always there when I defended arrogant and ignorant rulings I could not understand. I knew Doug was not now the boy who had released his adolescent passion in the body of his teen-age date. He was not the boy who let a minister splash him with water to please his grandmother or who let an angry father frighten him into a premature marriage. He was a serious young man who had discovered the meaning of life and loved a girl named Martha who agreed to share his dream. But Rome would not listen, my Church would not listen, and I sat speechless before this tragedy. I sat and watched them weep and walk away.

I had instructed Doug, told him the simplicity of my own faith, told him of a Christ Who spoke of mercy from a hill. I had watched his eyes grow soft, his mouth firm, as I read stories of the Gospel and reflected on their words. I remembered the night I spoke of the prodigal son, the boy who took his father's gift and squandered it in a land of emptiness and sin. I told him of the homecoming, when an aged father lifted a repentant man from his knees and held him in his arms, and called him "Son" again. I knew when I saw Doug's face that he was that "son" who had wandered in confusion and Korea until he found his Father's house. I knew the guilt that lurked in his memory and saw it relax when I spoke of Mary Magdalene. I loved the story and I told it with every passion I possessed. I recalled her loneliness, her morning sickness when she woke to find a stranger in her bed, the pain she felt at every hollow laugh, the longing for love, the ever-present fear of death.

And then I studied him when he heard that Magdalene discovered Christ, met a man who could love her without leering or clawing contemptuously at her body and her breasts, and she learned again to trust. And I knew Doug was Magdalene, the repentant Peter, the doubtful Thomas, the blind beggar, the leper in a cave, the dead young man who rose again to life. I saw him touch Martha's hand and knew that in his love for woman he had found his God. Without her my words were nothing, without her love there was no mystery of mercy and of Christ. He listened to me in the strength of her affection and heard me in the depths of her faithful love. And suddenly, in my office, on an evening I can't forget, I gave him the legal vision of my Church and murdered all his love. What could I say? "I'm sorry"? "Tough break, old man"? "Find another girl"? The prodigal son and Magdalene were frozen on my lips, and Doug and Martha turned and slowly walked away.

I do not exaggerate. I have stabbed a thousand brothers with the knife of law and watched the flowing blood. The names escape me in the mercy of time, but the faces, the expressions, the sad and despairing eyes remind me of the gore upon my hands. I remember the sallow introvert who grinned nervously in my office chair. He told me of his five-year marriage, from which he had recently escaped. His story came out haltingly as he told me of the wife who had made him impotent with her scorn and mockery. He had been married by a priest. But he had not had intercourse for fourteen months, not until one night after a parish picnic and half a case of beer. Then for three and a half years he had waited for her to come home with other men. He heard her laugh on the sofa downstairs, heard her moans of pleasure, heard her mock his vanished manhood as she settled in his bed.

Finally, he had left her before he would murder her in sleep. He had met another girl at work, a plain and gentle girl who made him know he was a man. He had felt the fire of passion for the first time in years and knew that he could have children of his own. He was in love, he could face himself again, and could begin to forget the wounds that had made him welcome death. So he came to his priest. He told his story and learned that one burst of semen had bound him to a whore. No priest could help him, no loophole could free him. He was just another baptized corpse to haunt me in my work. He left my office as sallow as he came, and paused politely at the door to thank me for my time.

No theology could support such madness. Theology, which once had tried to make the words of Christ a vital message in every age, had stood aside before the legal code. I knew no theology, I had never been taught. There was no theology in the seminary, only cubed thought, closed definitions, and narrow law. I was never asked to make a judgment; only a closed decision was handed me by men. I could not go to my bishop; he knew less theology than I. He had been carefully trained in canon law and protected his office by his knowledge of the minutiae of the legal code. He had surrounded himself with advisers who had completed graduate study in canon law. The degree of Doctor of Canon Law (JCD) is one of the most unusual examples of academic game-playing still to survive in our society. It has little to do with education and practically nothing to do with creative and theological thought. Yet the men who are trained in it would qualify any decision that I made.

I could not help the sallow man because Catholic theologians had been overrun by law. They did not speak out, and we can scarcely hear them now. They well know the horror of our legal-minded Church. They laugh at it in private, but they do nothing for the helpless parish priest and his suffering people who are too sad to laugh. They allow the vague rules, whose history tapers off in the twelfth century, to control the Catholic Church. They let a sallow and sorrowful man be destroyed by a rule that can be traced to a medieval scholar named Gratian, the honored Zeus of the canonical myth. They permit the sallow man to walk away in misery, bound by a law which says that semen seals a contract according to the ancient wisdom of Pope Alexander III or the mossy vision of one Hincmar of Rheims. And the legalist is so positive and so powerful, that the theologian prefers his words to Christ's.

God is not dead, Catholic theology is![1] And even the modern efforts are too feeble and too gentle to bring it back to life. The legalist rules! He is the man who solves every doubt by a new and narrow law. He insists on reducing every truth, no matter how complex, to the simple and manageable. He pouted at the Vatican Council and shackled the reformation of my Church. He frightens the bishops in their conferences and makes them quibble so they will not have to act. He binds the pastor, intimidates the parish priest. He can condemn a book without reading it, ban a movie without seeing it, and make a law without explaining it to men. And the theologian snarls in silence or is too frightened, too fond of preferment, too content to snarl at all. A bishop who has never read a book can force a theologian not to speak.

So the theologian is largely silent, or he deals with the simple and manageable truths that matter not to men. He, too, has become a legalist who runs from complexity, and gives the sallow man an answer which has no foundation in the testament of Christ. He lets the legalist rule and reduce every case of conscience to a clear and simple law. He lectures on the beauty of Christian marriage while the men of the streets hear nothing new but law. He lectures on the freedom of conscience while the simple sinners can't escape the law. He speaks of a democratic Church while the parishes flounder in grievances and pain. He asks for more time, for more thought, for deeper reflection, while the simple men, who cannot wait, are sentenced to misery and death.

Would he ask for time if his wife were weeping or his children driving him mad? Would he ask for time if he were losing the woman he loved, or living in fear of hell, or overwhelmed with bitterness he could scarcely control? Would he run from the legalist and ask for time if he could not pay his bills, or face his family, or quiet his screaming nerves? Christ did not ask for time to start a revolution, to challenge pharisees, to threaten the bullies who scandalized the troubled little ones. He called them "hypocrites," "vipers," "clean white coffins full of dead men's bones," and trusted men enough to let them love.

I hate the legalism of my Church. I hate what it has done to Catholics and what it has done to me. It tells me that I must pray my breviary an hour every day. It binds me under pain of sin, because it cannot believe that I will willingly give my time to prayer. But I hate the scheduled prayer that legalism imposes, the fat book of psalms and readings that I must complete. I am forced to read the dull and wordy speeches of men rather than to spend the time in silence with my God. I hate the loopholes that the legalist offers me to avoid this obligation, since such excuses only make me realize how unimportant is my prayer. He tells me that if I pay a few dollars to a missionary society, I will receive permission to say my rosary instead of my breviary when I drive a given distance in my car. But if I do not pay the money, I am bound to recite my boring breviary even if I drive my car. He told me this, and even as I hated him, I once assented to his words.

I hate the legalism that obliges me to anoint corpses with the holy oil of the last rites in hopes that a soul yet lingers in a cold body. I am embarrassed when the nurses pull back a sheet to reveal the withered flesh while I rub in my oil and whisper foreign words. It is superstitious magic, but the busy nurses soberly watch me out of pity or respect. In my heart I know I am wasting my time, that even if the body still nourishes life, the unconscious and dying man needs no oil of mine to lead him to his God. But I have forced myself to keep the law and to keep alive the simple ignorance that the Middle Ages handed modern Catholic men.

I condemn the legalist who can tell a Catholic that he must be married by a priest. I know the history of his law and realize that his kind once demanded, well into the eighteenth century, that even Protestants could only be married by a priest. I hate such arrogance, which forces Catholics to bring protesting Protestant spouses to the sanctuary of my Church, to ignore consciences and feelings, to blackmail simple men with the threat of no marriage unless they keep the smug, archaic rules. I hate the promises men of other faith must sign to take a Catholic bride. I hate the laws that can trample on Protestant tradition and wound the pride of Jews. But most of all I hate myself for keeping them.

I hate the legalism that tells a Catholic girl that her maid of honor must be a member of her Church. It is not enough that this witness to the wedding be a loyal friend who believes in marriage and the permanence of love. It is not enough that a best man be an honest man, but only that he be a Catholic no matter the weakness of his faith. I hate the law that tells Protestant grandparents that they cannot act as baptismal sponsors for their daughter's Catholic child. The very law of sponsors has no meaning, and in many cases, even an idle janitor will do. The priest's housekeeper can be summoned from her kitchen to witness legally the pouring of the water, and wonder what is happening to the pie that's in the oven. But a non-Catholic relative or friend cannot fulfill the law. Our legalists cannot even permit the parents to choose the child's name, but ask them to honor him with a proper patron saint. It does not occur to them that this tradition is outmoded, so loyal is their keeping of the law. To be called Mary is apparently more Christian than to be called Apple Blossom, unless, of course, "Apple" can be attributed to the saintly Apollonia, who died in innocence and peace.

I hate the legalism that teaches Catholics about indulgences and measures the amount of help that they can provide for purgatory's suffering souls.[2] It teaches that a three-word prayer is as valuable as seven years of public penance, so mighty is the spiritual treasury of the Church. And even though the theologian knows better, as does any man who thinks, the legalist controls our propaganda and leads our children on. He teaches them that prayers, said to gain an indulgence, must involve some motion of the lips. That will make them "public" as required by the law. He tells them that a series of indulgences can be gained only on successive visits to the Church, so obliges them to step momentarily outside the Church, then to return and pray some more. And the workmen obey, so do the nuns and priests, the doctors and professors, in loyalty to the legalism of their Church.

I hate the legalism that tells Catholics they cannot participate in the rites of another Church. I hate the narrowness and fear that forbid me to pray with Jews in their temple, to join the Methodists in their petitions and their hymns. I have not the nervous faith of the legalist who cannot look at the writings of other religions, who cannot challenge the doctrines of his Church. I can pray with any man, kneel with him, sing with him, share his communion or honor his belief. Only a legalist can ask me to love him with words while I shame him by the rudeness of my faith. He is as honest as I, and therefore as much in touch with God as I. And I will show him this by my respect for his faith even as I grow in the fulfillment of my own.

I despise the legalism that forbids a non-Catholic friend to receive communion in my Church.[3] I cannot call him brother if I will not share my food. The legalist tells me it would be sacrilegious for him to eat at my table, that this would make a mockery of God. The legalist runs a segregated restaurant, with a list of tawny rules, fixed firmly to the door. Only Catholics may come, only Catholics may eat, and they must be the Catholics whom he carefully approves. He stands as a snobbish headwaiter and ignores the hunger of the patrons who come without a tie.

I hate the legalism that preserves the ceremonies that have lost their meaning and explains the ancient rites that time has robbed of power to inspire men. I hate the legalistic wranglings in Rome that have made the prayers of Holy Week a bore. I watch the people on Good Friday and know their numbness as they listen to readings which are irrelevant and wearily say "Amen" to the endless petitions we should discard. I see them shuffle at the Easter Vigil as we chant over candles and water with dullness, and hurry through the dry selections from the Old Testament. I see them leave our churches in weariness and I detest the bureaucracy that will not give them what they need.

I reject the legalism that tells me I must support the Catholic schools to be loyal to my faith, the law that demands that Catholics support their Church while pastors erect expensive monuments to themselves. I despise the laws that tell a man to fast and do not permit him to select a penance that has some meaning in his life. And, most of all, I hate the legalism that forces Catholics to come each week to Mass, and then congratulates itself on the thriving life that packed pews and parking lots attest. It is this legalism that has forced hell to the fore of every Catholic conscience, that has muddled Catholic minds with the plenitude of sin.

And our poor, timid theology stands back and permits the

legalists to make madmen of us all. I hate the legalistic theology that can describe the angels and divide them all in choirs, that can name the devils and tell frightened men that evil spirits lure them into sin. It can make Adam's sin the source of sickness and death, his disobedience the cause of loneliness and unrestrained emotion. It can tell of limbo where the unbaptized babies go. It can package grace and measure all the mysteries that God has offered man. It can classify sins, enumerate the gifts of the Holy Spirit, order and arrange every virtue, name each attribute of God. It can make Christ so divine that he isn't human, his mother so marble that she cannot cry. It makes the Trinity into a course in logarithms, and turns the Apostles into a modern hierarchy. It tells me nothing new from eighth grade until I am ordained a priest, and does it with solemnity and dramatic frowns.

Legalism has drained our theology, enslaved our people, made hostile our non-Catholic friends. It permits bishops to stomp on priests, to ignore problems, to hoard money, to live in splendor, and to forget the poor. It permits pastors to destroy their assistants, to burden their people with the financial pressures born of personal appetite for prestige, to ignore the suffering of men, to mistreat nuns, to build a parish around their own convenience. It permits young priests to give sermons without preparation, to hear confessions with arrogance, to revel in undeserved praise, to escape blame, to remain immature, to grow ambitious, to avoid responsibility, to wither intellectually, to die emotionally, to drown in self-pity, to overlook the fears and feelings of men.

Legalism allows Catholics to feel holy when they are only docile, Christian when they are only the scrupulous observers of rules. It makes them proud that they are not Protestant, smug that they are free from sin. It causes them to boast about their mediocre schools, to exaggerate the evil in the world, to fear involvement, to take no action without the priest, to have no opinions without authority's support. It makes them suspicious, prejudiced, timid, blind to facts, disinterested in programs that do not serve the Church.

The legal mind is a restricted and impoverished mind which cannot move without a law to support each flicker of its brain. It is not satisfied to follow the norms of Christian love, or even to discover them in the romance of an involved life. The legalist laughs at such discovery, and calls an honest search for God a selfish and indulgent way of life. He only knows the way of law, and, for him, a Church which is not smothered in law is a religion without absolutes, a society without bones, a body without a spine. His way is the only way, even if millions tell him of their pain.

But we are Catholics, too, those of us who will not be bound by empty law. We will not abandon our Christ because a legalist says we must. We want living sacraments and not the tired forms that do not speak. We want a Mass that offers us food and love, and not a sterile ceremony that leaves us bored. We want to live by our conscience, to reflect on our experience, to hear the words of Christ, and not to be frightened into subjection by the cold force of law. We will not abandon our friends who feel obliged to practice birth control, who find peace in remarriage, who leave the priesthood for another way of life. We want a Church that will serve us in our search for happiness and fulfillment, and not smother us before we discover who we are.

We ask more of our Church than we ask of our government, more than we ask of industry, more than we ask of our parents and our home. We know that the Church is a society, that it must have its structure and law. But it cannot worship structures and multiply laws until man has no life or conscience of his own. Newman said it very well: "Conscience is a personal guide, and I use it because I must use myself; I am as little able to think by any mind but my own as to breathe with another's lungs. Conscience is nearer to me than any form of knowledge."[4]

Conscience is God's hand upon me, to restrain me, to lead me, to assure me that I am never lost, to convince me that I cannot live as every other man, to approve me when I do the honest thing. And my Church and I, my Church of the legal code, have labored long to tear men's consciences away.

I cannot heal the wounds I caused, nor calm the fears that I in honest ignorance forced upon the men I truly sought to help. I can only say I'm sorry, and promise never again to sell my conscience to the law. I cannot forget the woman of fifty who came to me in the parish church several years ago. She had been excommunicated from the Church because she had divorced her husband and married again. She had been living with her second husband, a non-Catholic, almost twenty years and heard from a friend that she could be reinstated if she promised not to have intercourse with him. She could cook his meals, wash his socks, make him laugh, share TV, but she could not join him in his bed. I told her that I would petition the bishop for this special privilege, called a "brother-sister arrangement," if she was sincere in her request. She thanked me with many tears and agreed to live this sexless life to know the joy of the sacraments of her Church.

Her petition was granted and she was informed that she could not receive communion in the parish Church, because there were people who knew the facts of her case. She insisted that this didn't matter and she would drive each Sunday to another town. She was also informed that this "privilege" could not promise her a burial in the Church. This hurt her deeply, and she made me promise that I would be at her funeral even if there was not a Mass to honor her in death.

For a few years I did not hear from her, and then one day she wrote me in the touching tones that indicate a fear of sudden death. She told me of the times that she had put her husband off when he came to her in bed. She told me of the confessions when the priest threatened to revoke her privilege if she broke her promise of celibacy again. She wrote of her longing to receive communion in the parish Church. But most of all she wanted the assurance that she could be buried from the Church. She did not want to die in disgrace or shame her children and her friends. So she wrote to me, the priest who got her the "privilege" she would never forget, the privilege that made her half a Catholic and half a wife.

I could not write her what my conscience suggested. I could

only give her the feeble comfort permitted by my Church. I told her she was not even sixty and death was most likely many years away. I told her that the Church might change its stand and that the modern debates in theology gave her a solid reason to hope. I felt sure that she could be buried in the Church.

But I could not tell her to be wife to the non-Catholic man who had lived with her for almost twenty years, who had fathered her two children and taken her out of town to Mass. I could not tell her to love him the way he wanted. I could not ask her to atone to him for the ignorance of her Church. I could only make promises for a funeral Mass when he couldn't have her any more. I could only make her his sister when he married her as his wife.

Now, however, I am not so frightened and I can write her from my heart:

I was wrong when I insisted that you make a brother out of that strong and noble man. I was wrong when I demanded that you abdicate his bed. Follow your heart and love him as your conscience will permit. I hope you can take him to yourself tonight, without guilt, without fear, and apologize for me, for you, for the arrogance of our Church. He is your husband if you believe he is, and the pen of a legalist cannot tear him from your side. Hold him close to you, he is kinder than most. Touch him gently, he has been wounded in his heart. If he has not taught you of God, then you will never learn. Make him your man, your husband, your strength, your contact with your God.

I will rest a little easier, knowing that you have joined him in his bed. But if you cannot be his wife until the Church offers you the chance, then so be it. But tell him that I wrote to you and read him what I said. And tell him I am sorry for the misery I caused. Then, at least, I may forget your tears, and his, and feel less a lawyer than a priest.

7. CONFESSION AND

MORTAL SIN

Whenever I take non-Catholic visitors through a Catholic Church, nothing arouses their curiosity like the confessional. They see it as a secret little room hidden in the corner of the Church where Catholics come and whisper their sins and failures to the priest. They think of their own sins, and wince at the thought of revealing them to anyone. I try to move to other items of interest in the church, but the visitors' glance is fixed on the confessional. They remember the stories they have heard, the movies where priests confronted criminals or sinful women in dramatic confessions, and the fears of their Catholic friends who felt compelled to get to confession before a Saturday date.

Catholics, however, take the confessional in stride. They seldom question its value or significance, presuming that there is no other satisfactory way to find peace of conscience and freedom from sin. They love it and hate it, fear it and praise it, rush to it regularly or stay away for years. It has offered them peace and fulfillment, discouragement and bitterness, but it is at the heart of their Church's structure. Seldom do they forget it, no matter how far they wander from the Church. They know it is a sacrament, a sacred ritual which offers them God's forgiveness in tangible form. It is not merely the therapy of self-accusation, nor the comfort of vanished guilt. It is a symbolic contact with God, the sense of His presence and absolving hand. It is a mystery entrusted to sinful men to extend in time the love and mercy of God.

Catholics believe that Christ established this sacred ritual of forgiveness and encouragement. It is the court of appeals where the sinner's own honesty is the only jury, his own conscience the ultimate judge. The woman in adultery comes here to reveal the weakness that her husband would never understand. The angry adolescent comes to confess the contempt for his father he fears to admit to his closest friend. The alcoholic comes when his wife and children have turned their backs, when his employer has lost his patience, and his friends merely nod and back away. The single girl comes to explain the affair that would kill her mother if she knew; the homosexual comes when parents are disgraced and doctors cannot help; the little boy comes to whisper in fear his first awareness of the sexual urge. Young and old come to find forgiveness for their "mortal sins."

Mortal sin, to a Catholic, is a serious offense which severs man's friendship with God. It is "the greatest evil in the world," more serious than Vietnam, more final than death, more tragic than the murder of a child. It can descend like lightning into the life of peasant and president alike. It is not an infrequent occurrence in the lives of Catholics, although it usually reserves its fury for certain stress periods in life. Adolescence is such a period. The Catholic teen-ager lives in the shadow of mortal sin. He knows the three simple conditions for its fearful presence: a serious matter, sufficient reflection and awareness of the evil deed, and full consent of the will. When these three conditions are present, a single action leaves man in a state of rejection by God. Were he to die while in this state, he would know the pain of an eternal hell. He could utter no plea in his own behalf, the time for excuses and reforms would be over, and he would burn forever in misery and regret.

The conditions are not too easy to apply. But the sinner refuses to take a chance. The odds are too great. He might wonder if missing Mass or masturbating[1] is really very wrong. He might question the seriousness of his passionate fondling of his girl friend, or the drinking party that provoked the neighbors to summon the police. He might even debate with himself the extent of his awareness, or the freedom he possessed at the time of his sin. He might search for excuses, recall the state of mind that drove him, the circumstances that precipitated his behavior. Probably, however, he will run to confession as quickly as he can lest he risk the sudden death that would summon him to hell.

The average Catholic learns from his youth the agony of guilt, and will struggle with its pangs through college and business, through retirement and terminal illness. While he has heard that confession is a sacrament of gentle mercy, it is often to him a tense ritual of anxiety and guilt. While he comes as the prodigal son, he often faces an angry executioner instead of an understanding father. Theoretically, he knows what confession *should* mean in terms of confidence and peace, but practically it *does* mean a life immersed in guilt. The exceptional may well escape such suffering because they have conquered or repressed the human drives which make of confession the feeding ground of guilt. They are not living in conscious fear of hell, because their sins are the gentle violations of impatience and neglected prayers. They come to confession to receive a merit badge, to hear the congratulations of the priest. But the rest of us, the sinners, the weak and confused, the human and passionate, come to whisper our mortal sins to the priest. We sense his anger, feel his hostility, endure his sermons, and dare not question his naïve solutions to the temptations we face.

We come because we have learned from childhood that confession is the only safe way to escape mortal sin. We have been taught that God will indeed forgive us without confession— but on two conditions: if our sorrow is "perfect," that is, if it stems from our concern for the injury we have done God rather than our fear of going to hell; and if our delay in confession is not due to procrastination. We are never certain, however, of the "perfection" of our sorrow until we have received the forgiveness of the priest. I can remember as a boy, when I gave in to the weakness of my flesh, trying desperately to speak my "perfect" sorrow, only to live in misery until I went to confession. Then, for a moment, I knew exhilaration and hope, only to flounder in guilt when another temptation flattened me in "mortal sin."

I can well understand, as a priest, the college boy who called me at midnight and asked for confession before he dared sleep. He came to my office in a state of almost hysterical fear. He sobbed like a little child, tried to tell me what had happened, but only wept the more. Finally, he calmed himself enough to tell me his "mortal sin" with obvious regret. He had been petting with his girl friend. Usually she had pushed his hand away. This night, however, she had been as "weak" and curious as he. He assured me that they had not gone "all the way," but realized that they were now in "mortal sin." He had returned home, struggled with his conscience, and called me to free him from his sin. I knew the forgiveness I offered would give him a night's rest. I tried to talk to him, to assure him that he had done nothing so terrible, but the fears learned in childhood blotted out my words. He only wanted forgiveness, and begged for it, came too frightened to be ashamed of what I might think. He felt obliged to tell me each passionate motion of his hand, each fleshly sensation, to describe his ardor in each intimate detail. And when I forgave him, he sobbed his thanks, told me I was the "greatest," and strode happily away. But he would be back.

And this young man is no exception in our system. He is the preview of the anxious adult who rushes to confession to escape the fire of hell. He is one in a series of frightened sinners who come to reveal their "mortal sins." Most of the mortal sins they bring center around Mother Lust and her numberless children. There are the "impure thoughts and "impure desires" which are "mortal" only if they are nourished and embraced. This distinction requires the sinner to decide precisely when they are "nourished and embraced." The Catholic conscience avoids the dilemma by "playing it safe" and confessing to the priest. Then there is "petting," which includes the sexual touch, and "necking," which covers untold varieties of abortive love-making. Again, the ordinary man dares not fool with the fires of hell, so he assembles his "sins" like a giant grocery list and checks them off in turn. Marriage brings its own "mortal sins," and the Catholic hardly returns from the honeymoon before the conscience wrangling starts again.

There are, of course, mortal sins on our books which do not center on sex. The only one that occurs with any frequency is that of missing Mass. In addition, each conscience will have its special sin that keeps it in turmoil. There are prepared lists of sins around many Catholic churches to help the sinner decide what separates him from God. Such lists dissect the commandments and challenge the want ads for compact information. Visits to fortunetellers are lined up with false oaths and superstitions. Then come profane speech, and warnings to the nagging wife and stubborn child, to brawlers, drunkards, and thieves, to the doubters, the despairers, and the suicide-seekers who lost their nerve. Even charity, which once was the motif of every Christian law, is perforated into a dozen little species of rancor and deceit. Not all the sins on the list are "mortal," but each Catholic seems to have his own version of the boundary between "mortal" and "venial" sin. No amount of instruction, for example, can convince Mike that it is not a "mortal sin" to say "God damn it" when the Yankees lose to Boston in the ninth.

Most Catholic Churches cater to the troubled conscience of their children. Confessions are heard with great regularity.[2] Some parishes offer confessions every evening; others, during morning Mass. Nearly every parish lines up its penitents on Saturday afternoon and evening to permit the guilt-ridden people to return to their weekend in peace. Each person is given approximately a minute, unless he happens to be a stray sheep who returns or a sinner who is involved in a problem of sex. The confessional is swamped at Christmas and Easter, and priests may well listen to the whisper of sin for a dozen hours a day. But no matter when the light of the confessional signals the priest's readiness to absolve the weakness of men, no matter the day or the hour, the people appear.

Some, however, do not come. Some are too terrified to recite their secret sins, so they live in guilt instead. Some grow discouraged and give up on confession. Others postpone it until a time when they hope they will be better able to live within the narrow boundaries of the Catholic conscience. They stay away and try to ignore the stinging reminders from the pulpit, hoping they will not be stricken with unexpected death. Many, indeed, do not come, but few escape the fear that was nourished in their mind from childhood and troubles them whenever they think of God.

It is hard to relate such routine guilt and organized forgiveness to the gospel of Jesus Christ. Our confessional becomes a travesty when we compare it to the Christian vision of pardon. Christ promised freedom and we offer imprisonment and guilt.[3] Christ spoke of joy and we offer only a break in tension to be followed by a more painful relapse. Christ gave us a new direction and we provide a sacred automaton which binds the very heart it promises to release. We don't offer hope or confidence or love. We don't help a man to understand his weakness or encourage him to be patient and to grow. We tell each man that he is uniquely sinful, and we urge him to produce an ideal self which is likely years away. We permit his guilt to mount on the strength of his repeated failures and we teach him to resolve with spiritual help[4] problems which are emotional in origin. We beat him down when he needs a hand to lift him from his pain. We ask him to be a robot when he tries to tell us he is a man of flesh and blood. He comes for understanding and the courage to endure; we treat him with coldness and routine dispatch.

And despite our abuse, he is helpless. We have carefully taught him, simple or sophisticated, that there is no place else to go. He is bound in the guilt we taught him, and held to the narrow forgiveness we provide. He comes to Christ and he hears an impersonal voice. I do not see him when I hear his confession. I do not know his background, his circumstances, his pain. I only hear his whisper and docile acceptance of everything I say. He dares not argue with me, he dares not even tell me of the progress he notes. He tells me his sins, waits for my judgment, and rushes out to admit another of the waiting sheep. He even thanks me as he leaves, because he has not the confidence to find peace without the comfort of my absolution. I am the only one who can free him from his mortal sins and make it possible for him to live without the ever-present fear of hell.

He does not know that theologians are presently questioning the very notion of "mortal sin."[5] He may not hear of such valid speculation for another dozen years. Yet the best of our theologians well know that we cannot justify our childish vision of mortal sin. It has been too easy to sever one's friendship with God. Such a vicious conception of God as we have known makes of our Creator a Prussian general or an angry Irish judge. It sees "mortal sin" everywhere and makes of life a tightrope on the brink of hell. The Catholic only knows that a single Mass not attended because of weariness can be a mortal sin. This makes little sense, though the average Catholic is too frightened to reflect.

Who can love the God of this theology, the God Who can dismiss His friends with such readiness and ease? Even weak men do not break their friendship with one another without long and serious cause. If God is so sudden in His judgment and so petulant in His anger, who could take Him seriously or hope to win His love? One argument does not break our relationship with a friend. Nor does a single act of greed or egotism or self-indulgence ordinarily tear our hearts apart. A friend accepts an excuse, and under no circumstances would he destine us to hell.

Our notion of mortal sin is as sick as any element of our theology. It presumes that when man acts he is in complete possession of himself, that he can contain his whole personality in a single act. But how often in human life can a single act build or destroy a friendship? How often does any man perform a "centered action," a truly "self-representing deed"? Love is built through a thousand experiences. It is compounded of laughs and tears, gentle forgiveness and secret fears, boredom, a new baby, a lost job, a miscarriage, a hundred midnight snacks, days when communication suffers, nights when a common pillow cannot create unity, and other days and nights when the flow of hearts is free.

A man cannot stand back after a week or ten days and say: "How is our love?" He cannot evaluate a marriage or a friendship by a temper tantrum or an occasional cycle of discouragement or emptiness. He can only rely on the thousand fibers that wove a love to sustain it from the wear of routine and rebuff. Love will fight closeness as often as it will seek it out. Man cannot even measure or chart his love; there is no way to reduce it to a list of rules or a graph with peaks and valleys. Only occasionally can he look back and sense that he and his wife have been growing apart or that his dread of failure has made him tense and irritable, or that his restlessness has taken him from his duties as husband and father. Only over a year or two can a couple recognize that artificial appetites for status and social prominence have cooled a friendship. Even then they do not panic, but attempt to move gradually onto another plateau of love. Not every argument can become a crisis and demand a formal retraction of angry words or selfish indulgence. Mature love has more confidence than that. It does not have to make "firm and sudden resolves" or "absolute promises of amendment." It has some respect for itself and simply takes a step forward without looking back. Least of all does it try to remember the name and number of each offense and to report it in a confession to be reviewed in domestic court.

Why should man's relationship with God be different? Why should confession have to be a detailed list of thoughts and actions, and not merely a calm and general appraisal of life with a burst of new hope for the future?[6] Why must a man report each serious sin in number and kind, and not merely indicate the direction and growing maturity of his love? Why must he be frightened from his childhood with the philosophy of "Better be safe than sorry"? It is only a moral theology steeped in legalism and casuistry that has required confession to be more like an income tax report than a personal contact with the holy God. If a person were only expected to make a private confession on rare and important occasions, and not after every individual "mortal sin," then confession could be truly personal. The priest could be a person and not an absolving machine. The penitent could be a person and not an irritating whisper in a long gray line. A kind of general confession could be held on regular occasions, whereby a man could confess his faults silently to God and hear the forgiveness provided for all the people in the name of Christ.

The format of private confession would change. There would be no need for anonymity (though it could be had), nor would there be any need for the production-line approach. The Catholic prefers anonymity because he is forced to list the details of embarrassing sins, and is made to think that his sins are unusual and sordid. He would not want anonymity if he could discuss the realities of his life and hopes, and talk with a priest who is human enough to understand. I have heard numerous private confessions in this "open" way during college retreats, and the numbers of penitents kept me busy far into the night.

Recently I gave a retreat at a Catholic college. I offered a new approach to confession which did not bother with lists of sins or embarrassing details. I told the students of my own struggles with the sins of the flesh that trouble every man. I insisted that each man shares our weakness and that no one of us can judge another's guilt. I asked that they not be too hard on themselves, that they not stay away from communion or confession because they could not achieve total reform. The results of such confessions were exciting. The students had formerly found confession as dull and meaningless as I. They hated to go as strongly as I hated to hear their lists of sins. Suddenly, confession began to make sense, and the students, long denied a hearing by the Church, continued to come for several days and nights.

The procedure was simple. We just sat and talked, and at times smoked a cigarette. It was far from a "Bless me, Father, here are my sins" approach. It was a conference about the things of the spirit and the hopes of a person. I asked for no details, although often enough they discussed comfortably even the problems of marriage and courtship, or their concern with the emptiness of modern life. I didn't sit as the judge of personal conscience, since no man has such a right. I was only the judge of sorrow and our presence together made such a judgment unnecessary. We merely talked about the goals of courtship and marriage, the secret dangers of self-deception and of self-indulgence masquerading as love. We talked of the difficulty of prayer in modern society, of the hunger for money and success, of the indifference which infects young minds faced with a term of duty in Vietnam. I shared with them some of my own experience, and that of the many people with whom I had worked. I did everything but read to them from the gory lists of traditional sins. Most of all, I listened,[7] and for the first time in my life, I began to understand what confession could mean. I heard young hearts screaming to find relevance in our Mass and sacraments. I heard honest doubts about the dogmas which had been inherited, but never embraced. After our confession, we knelt down together in the presence of God and I asked His forgiveness in the name of Christ.

I had not heard the confessions, for once, of the gentle girls whose only dates were with eagle scouts on tennis courts on sunny afternoons. Nor had I heard only of sex and anger for a change. I heard the doubts of those who wondered if communion could possibly produce a change in character. I heard valid questions about the worth of religious education. I heard about pressures from home and the secret fears of the lonely, the deep prejudices, the hatred for parents, the tales of honor students who came to school, and remained there only to please an ambitious father or mother. I heard men and women talking to a man and heard dozens tell me that they had rediscovered their faith.

Catholics are ready for confession in such a framework. They are sick of playing games and running to different confessors to whisper regularly their secret sins behind silent screens. They are tired of a morality which can chart their acts before they begin, and can treat extenuating, simply human circumstances as if they did not exist. Confession has become a public bath with a single bar of soap and a common towel, and modern young Catholics are growing to ignore it with maturity and experience. They are demanding a confession which offers them a chance to be a person.

I can hear the legalists tell me about the *objective* moral law. I can even watch the traditional theorems working in the pulsing of their veins. And yet I know that morality can never be universally imposed. It can only be the growing experience of an individual, and short of this is mere conformity.[8] Even the scholastics have seen morality as the "moral quality of a personal act," and, as such, it cannot be univocally enforced. Morality and moral views depend largely on knowledge and experience, and I cannot tell this young man or woman what intercourse before marriage means to every Christian. I can only ask what it means to him or her. If purity, in the legalistic and traditional sense, means nothing but a game to this person, then it is no longer purity, but only mute compliance with a law that belies experience. This does not mean that I agree with him, it does not even mean that he is certain of his own position. It only means that together we are attempting to measure this relationship in terms of God and human love. It only means that he has a chance to grow, to make mistakes, to become himself.

We have never been able to talk to Catholics about goals in confession. We have never been able to talk about anything except to comment on a tailored recitation of "sins." For this reason we have often not reached them where they felt, but only where they said they thought. We talked to them in quiet groups without dialogue, and even when we had them alone in confession, we were satisfied with a routine recalling of the accepted sins. We did not teach them to be responsible to God, only to be accountable to us.

A mathematical confession without dialogue permits the priest to absorb the conscience of the person. It prevents the individual from achieving honest self-knowledge. He may well be satisfied to confess the same way for twenty years, still accusing himself of "swearing thirty times," "fighting with his wife eleven times," and "thinking dirty thoughts about women a dozen times—more or less." Meanwhile he may be organized

to keep Negroes out of his neighborhood, play at a golf course
that blackballs Jews, and value every human relationship in
terms of money or personal prestige. Simply to tell his sins and
to promise reform can be a simplistic and self-centered search
for "personal holiness." Man becomes holy with someone else,
and only when he begins to recognize his responsibility to the
"other," the "thou," is he even capable of the religious experience—no matter the frequency and the accuracy of his confessions.

Obviously, such a personal, truly individual confession as I
propose could not be made frequently, nor would it be required.
General confessions in a group would provide a man with the
needed opportunity to express his sorrow regularly and to know
the power of his victory in the risen Christ. In such a confession the person would confess his sins silently to God and hear
the public words of forgiveness spoken in the name of Christ.
The private confession could be held by appointment at special
times (as it frequently is in the Episcopal Church). Sometimes
it might not be needed for years, or at other times it might be
needed every couple of months. The Catholic people, long
trained in the fearful theology of mortal sin, would have to be
conditioned for such new freedom, but it would not take as
long as some may think. Recently, for example, I gave a day of
recollection to a group of sisters. The superior and I had an
honest talk. She told me her views on confession and they were
surprisingly like my own. She told me of the painful routine of
weekly confession and the indifference she felt toward the confessor who had heard her sins for almost four years. Gradually,
she had grown old enough or wise enough to call a halt to this
programmed boredom. Presently, she goes to confession only
when she feels the need or comes in contact with a priest who
can reach her in a special and human way. After years of indifference, confession has meaning for this honest nun.

Priests, of course, might object that they have neither the
time nor the counseling ability for such an approach to confession. But the priest would have time—the endless hours he
currently spends hearing the confessions of the fearful and

guilt-ridden. He would have time if he were permitted to be a servant of the word and the sacraments, and not a fund raiser, a teacher of high-school Latin, a band director, a bazaar chairman, a bingo caller, and the emergency entertainer at the ladies' guild when Betty Crocker doesn't show up. The priest may well lack the techniques of dialogue, since his education taught him to be a part-time pope and sublime inquisitor. He could, however, be taught. He could learn something of the dynamics of personal interview and dialogue, and learn a great deal about human motivation and the ingredients that compose a person. He would have to discipline himself to learn to listen more than he talks. He would have to understand that no one can impose moral views on another, and that life is a process of growth and not a large vacuum that collects the infallible conclusions of medieval theologians. He would even have to acquire respect for the ideals of his own society, and if he ever assumed the role of prophet-critic, he would reveal that he was as much a man of his own day as a resounder of Christian tradition. Especially would he have to learn to believe in man and to know that the greatest asset in man's search for Christ is the very human heart that God has fashioned in His own image.

The priest could even have a better picture of man if he were not tied to a tired and impossible vision of the original sin of Adam. Original sin, in its traditional expression, is the sin of Adam which all men have inherited. The priest, and all Catholics, have learned that this inheritance made of the prize product of God's creation a limping and wounded lover living on the fringe of self-deception and divine fury. Man was not destroyed by Adam, in the accepted view of the Eden myth, but would be the eternal puppet of passion and ignorance. He was doomed to death, and even after baptism had put him on the road of life, he would wear the tearful scars of Adam's betrayal.

The theology of original sin has moved a long way from Augustine's view that it was passed through the union of parents who bore their children in the fire of carnal love.[9] Most of such progress in theological thought, however, has taken place within the last five years. We are beginning to recognize that Adam is only a symbol of man, the concrete embodiment of man's struggle to discover love amid the feebleness of the flesh and the loneliness of the spirit. Original sin is the sin of a world that crucified Christ and rejects His way of peace for a life of anxiety and isolation.[10] It cannot point to a single pair of parents nor blame a curious man and woman in a mythical garden. It cannot be contained in a solitary act of disobedience, but can only gradually be seen in the gathering anger and hatred of men. One must stand back to see it in the wars and massacres of man, in the violence of the cities and the pillage of the countries. It can be seen in the father who loves his family even as he runs from them, or hurts them, or draws their very blood. It can be seen not as a static and historic offense, but as a dynamic reality dividing man himself even as it divides the world. It can grow when man teaches man distrust and hatred, and can wane when man embraces man in love. It is the sin of a world, not of a single parent, the groan of a creature who is expected to be a creator even as he whines like an animal to be left in isolation.

In a society of superstition and pseudoscience, the myth of Adam's indulgence of Eve could answer each question about the origin of evil and death. In such a world evil had to have parents even as thunder and lightning were tied to some magical source. But we do not live in such a world. We know that the authors of Genesis knew nothing of "original sin,"[11] but only recognized sadly that man could deny bread to his hungry brother and kings could sleep with maidens who had not the freedom to protest. They knew that evil was in the world and they only said that it was not the creation of the holy God. They saw it as a kingdom to itself, with its prince of darkness and its code and covenant and gods of metal and stone. Even in Christian times, Paul would speak of evil as if it had arms and legs and the crown of a perverted king.[12] He did not hesitate in his *Letter to the Romans* to borrow the Adam symbol and to make of it a striking contrast to the liberating Christ. Paul was not interested in tracing the family tree of sin and hatred; he only wanted to announce that man had new causes to rejoice in the victory of the risen Christ. He, with all of his reputation for anti-feminism and sexual anxiety, was a herald of victory and not a messenger of sin's supremacy. Paul saw Christ as a beginning, the promise of triumph, the pledge of new growth, the bearer of "good news" to an unhappy world, the trumpet sound of victory.

After twenty centuries of "victory," the battle is not yet won. Nor will it be until the world is no more. The "original sin," man's fear of love, remains, and yet each new generation can sense a growing freedom from its power. Our parents have known its force and passed it on, but we live with the hope that it will not reign as actively in our own lives. We believe that our personal struggle to love will be reflected in the lives of our children, as "original sin" loses more of its fury with each step forward that man takes in creative love. No man can measure the evil of his generation, nor can he accurately compare it with a world in which he did not live. But if Christianity means anything, and is not merely a single and passing state of man's development, it must mean that we have edged forward a step with the love that our parents transmitted to us.

Our parents left us evil as well, such as the deep-seated prejudices which they acquired in fear and ignorance. They left us insecurities that we conquer only with difficulty. They left us intolerance and superstition, shortsightedness and insensitivity. They left us quarrels with our brothers, desperately unresolved. They left us distrust of the world and its joys. They left us "original sin," and we shall, unwittingly, pass it on to the children we have been called to love. We cannot look back and blame an historic Adam for his feeble resistance to a snake's request. We can only look to a kind of man that lives in every man, the man whose "demon" conquers his spirit, the man who knows even as he falls that he can and must rise. I am such a man, and so are you, and together we have crucified Christ when we ignore the power of His resurrection. This is the remnant of the "original sin."

Such a view of original sin makes the mystery of mortal sin

less obscure. The true "mortal sin," the true sin of death, is that human existence which approves Christ's death by the consistent refusal to love. Perhaps such a sin can be committed in a single act, but rarely is man so in possession of himself that he can endorse Calvary by missing Mass, or acting "impurely," or shutting out his wife and children. Perhaps after a year, or several months, he can look back on his life and know that his goal, his "ultimate concern" has been unworthy of a child of God. He must, however, recognize the "evil" he has done. We ask too much of man when we see a rejection of God in a burst of passion or fear or bitterness. And if man himself cannot agree that his action cuts him off from God, how can he be held responsible? How can a single act send him to hell? Love is not a single act, nor is its loss. The moral theology that handed us our view of mortal sin and forced us to run trembling to confession was based upon a medieval vision of man. Such a vision has passed, as should our archaic description of sin.

Catholic theology has made too much of Adam's sin and not nearly enough of Christ's victory.[13] We learned well enough that it might take us years to "grow up" in Christ, but we ignored the development necessary to be named one of Satan's recruits. No reasonable theologian would say that a single act of love binds us to God in eternal fervor. Even the great conversions of Christian history were the climax of a thousand victories. How can the same theologians be so facile in cutting off the creature from his Creator in the throes of a lonely act?

The Christian must know that he is a conqueror, a man of undiminished hope, the only son of a loving Father Who does not arbitrarily reject in pettiness and petulance. How many times have I heard the weariness of the world in hours of confession and known that these were not sons but slaves? How many times did I hear the people confess to "feel better" when I well knew that they would never feel anything but fear and temporary relief from fear until they learned that Christ had conquered Adam? To abstain from the communion table because there is no chance to confess a "mortal sin," to hurry to report each solitary sin and "impure embrace" is to make of the

Christ of Magdalene and Peter a pompous judge in a traffic court. To call "sinful" what one's own heart says is good and holy is to refuse to be a man. To count each sin and classify it in a moral computer is to make a mockery of a sacrament of mercy.

I cannot hear such confessions any longer. I cannot fight sleep and boredom as men file by and formally list their basketful of faults. I cannot bear their guilt over trifles, their repentant reports of the "sins" that are merely the story of a maturing soul. I am tired of taking away sins that I cannot be certain exist, of evoking promises that cannot be kept, of representing a God Who so easily sentences men to hell.

Once on a hillside in Galilee man saw another Man Who spoke of God. He did not multiply laws as the Pharisees, or wrangle in subleties like the Sadducees. He did not cross-examine or condemn like the courts of Rome. He seemed to understand, to believe in man, to realize that beneath this shy smile and wrinkled glance rested the image of His own Father. He carried neither pencil nor pad, nor adding machine to tabulate the offenses of men. He spoke of a son who could always come home, a helpless lamb that would tremble in fear until it heard His voice.

We need such a man in the Catholic Church today, a man who understands and bleeds to forgive, a man who will take our word even if we are only halfway to honesty, a man who will not call "sinful" what we can only see as a necessary step in the search of love. We need to find the light and joy that was lost in the legalism of history's dust and decay. We need to find priests again, priests who can make men's hearts glow with confidence in themselves, and not mere absolving robots who hand out green stamps to the frightened children. Then will the Church have something to say to the man of our generation, when the confession line dwindles and the invitation to the banquet reaches the poor, the weak, the truly human. Then can my Church, grown cold and formal, speak the words that made men follow: "Come to me, you that labor and are burdened, and I will give you rest."

8. THE RULES OF
COURTSHIP

It is always disconcerting to hear the retreat questions of a senior in a Catholic girls' college. We could well discuss the new opportunities that modern psychology offers in raising well-loved children. We could talk about the signs of love or the breakdown in personal communication. We could even talk about the sorry preoccupation of the fair sex with bustlines and hiplines. There is so much to talk about with a sincere and sophisticated young lady approaching career and marriage. But we always seem to end up with an incredibly naïve and tiresome discussion about "French kissing" or "prolonged embracing." If the results of her formation were not so sad and unfortunate, the whole conversation would be comical.

Her education has taken her from the first suggestions of Euclid to the last offerings of Einstein. She has read Teller and Wittgenstein, Tillich and Graham Greene. Her vision, however, of the moral meaning of sex and love has hardly progressed since grade nine. Every date has been a natural, human exchange until the last drop of coffee has been drained from the cup and the bewitching hour approaches. Then the wheels begin to spin in their mathematical track. To kiss or not to kiss is hardly the question, though once it well may have been a decision matching marital consent in its gravity. To French

kiss or not to French kiss is usually the question. Keeping the
teeth closed becomes the ancient badge of the martyrs who refused to sacrifice to the pagan gods of Rome. She has undoubtedly heard from priestly lips that the "soul kiss" is a symbol of
intercourse, and she has bowed to the logic of one who may
have kissed no one other than his mother. At times she would
like to spring loose from a system of morality which measures
hugs and times kisses, but her fear of hell's fire sends her back
into line.

One gentle touch of curious hands, one burst of passion
that pulls her body too close to his, and she wonders about the
next opportunity for confession. In a society in which the
"French kiss" is a normal way to express affection, she firms
her lips and guards her tongue with all the ardor of a convent
under siege. From a quiet conversation over coffee, she has
galloped to a state of scrupulous frenzy in twenty minutes.
Maybe she shouldn't see him again; after all, they really haven't
made plans for marriage. She likes him, but she is not yet prepared to commit herself for life. She's playing the field, and
the only time she is comfortable is the very first date with a
very shy young man. She has heard of men who take girls to
their stereophonic apartments and the sad tales of pregnant
friends who took a prolonged tour of "Europe." She had heard
the retreat talks that start with the Immaculate Conception and
end with drive-in movies and broken homes. She has heard so
much more about sex than about love that love becomes an un-
attainable ideal and sex the forbidden path that leads to misery.

Since the age of twelve she has heard about the dangers of
the hayride and necking parties where twelfth-grade boys
threaten the virginity of giggling girls. She has been told that
her body is a Temple of the Holy Spirit and that a kiss is a
sacred symbol of deep affection. By the time she was in ninth
grade she probably knew the difference between necking and
petting, and wondered when her first encounter would threaten
her faith and morals. For years she had been confessing regularly her "bad" thoughts and "impure desires," and the passage
of time meant only that the cinema of imagination offered her

more to worry about. She learned that she was a gentle daisy in a grisly, leering world. Her little Protestant friends, with their whispers and knowing grins, would soon enough discover the horrors of unprincipled living. They were not burdened with the great charter of sexual mores and their experiential approach to libido would punish them in marriage. Yet, because it doesn't always turn out that way, the Catholic system cannot afford to highlight the successful marriages of the morally unenlightened. Purity in the form of total abstinence is the proof of love, according to the Catholic view, even though "purity" can also be proof of neurotic guilt or fear of physical love. Augustine suggested to the violated virgins of his *City of God* that they were able to remain humbly pure, since savage barbarians had stolen their physical virginity. The Catholic ethos, however, is timid in drawing conclusions from such bold speculations. Since there are enough quotes from Augustine to enforce the most puritan system of morality, his advice to the blushing virgins has gone the weary way of his "Love and do what you will"— paraphrased out of existence.

In any event, Augustine has had little to do with the Catholic conscience, which has found nourishment enough in such Jesuitical offerings as Kelly's *Modern Youth and Chastity*. Here the rules are all laid out in handy fashion. Even the first kiss of the sweaty-fingered sophomore is categorized. Five rules, practically impossible of application, are listed to cover "every" situation. First, the Catholic has to know what "venereal pleasure" is. It would seem hard to define, but rather easy to experience. It is not a simple love glow or the moon-tingling sensation of dancing with a wind-blown pinafore of starched cotton. It is passionate, intense, violent! Venereal pleasure is always seriously wrong for the unmarried, whether "direct" or "proximately indirect." Try this for size on a fourteen-year-old conscience!

Venereal pleasure is distinguished from the more gentle varieties known as affection. Affection is legitimate if it is sincere. The violations of the rules on affection are not considered serious, and, for the confused Catholic conscience, this means, "Don't sweat it!" The line, however, between affection and venereal pleasure is the narrow boundary between dark white and light black. It is so easy to slip from the gentle brush of tender lips to the torrid embrace of locked arms. Prolonged kissing is usually presumed to be "passionate," and passionate kissing is the entryway to lust. The question that naturally flows from this profound speculation is: "When is a kiss prolonged?" A quick check of the medieval minds is not a great help. Some suggest that twenty seconds might be prolonged. Others, more practical, think that passionate kissing is marked by the gradual replacing of a love purr with a bearish growl. No effective formula has been devised to determine the moral quantity of a hug. Weary moralists, like myself, have usually ended all discussion with the weak assurance that "You'll know when it happens." At least, I hoped they would, since I had never known myself. The closest I came to a passionate embrace in my preseminary days was a ten-minute ride in the back seat of a crowded car after a football game. My formation was quite average in seminary circles.

Our intentions are not bad. People need much help in facing life's wonders. Sexual experience can be as dangerous as it is beautiful. We need goals, self-questioning, some understanding of the heterosexual dynamic. Girls need to know something about the psyche of man, as well as the inner activities of their own psyche. Young men need to know the characteristics that divide male and female, and the danger of calling a passionate experience an undying love. There is a lifetime of learning, but it cannot be contained in neat categories. In reducing a profound area of human experience to a set of rules, we somehow manage to take away the conscience of the young Catholic and substitute the sexual hangup.

Young Catholics learn to guard their thoughts and to banish lustful desires.[1] They often complain that such efforts are futile, and the more they banish, the more fruitful seems the supply. Teen-agers are of especial concern. They report their passionate kissing, their "almost petting," their brief and furtive touches, their moments of curious excitement. They want to be sure. They do not think this act is "mortal," but the odds are too great to take a chance. The more conscientious torture us with the stuttering distinctions that our moral code has made so essential.[2] They want to know the borderline of mortal and venial sin, they probe to discover how far they can go—to drain each ounce of pleasure and experience without offending God. Nothing seems serious in confession except matters of sex. We hear of quarrels at home, struggles with sullen friends, bits of theft and disobedience—but it is only sex that brings hoarse fear to the voice and concern to the confessor's admonitions.

In such a world, "going steady" is the most fertile target of our attacks. We condemn the steady daters whenever we can. We expel them from school, call them in for private council, telephone their parents, and dissect them in our religion class. We try every new vaccine to end this blight, yet nothing seems to work. We are nostalgic and tell them of our old gang, where no one went steady. Why can't modern youth gather around the piano, or linger around the redolent smoke of the autumn hot-dog roast? We had so much fun in "our" day, when guys and gals traveled in packs, and there was little time or place to linger in private passion. We extoll the athlete and mock the twisting teen who lets his id run wild in an orgy of discordant sounds. We criticize the public schools, where skinny boys hold hands with listless girls between classes. We whisper about the scandals of the locker rooms and dark alcoves. We hear of teachers who treat promiscuity as a joke. We are the enlightened, and we demand that our young prepare themselves for marriage with discipline and honor.

The results of our campaign have not been exceptional. We still have our surprise pregnancies, our premature marriages, our little parties that help make clear the distinction between affection and venereal pleasure. Some of our young come back to us in confession and tell us of their exciting misdeeds. Some do not, but instead postpone confession until such a time as their repentance will have some roots. Few give up their new experience, even if it means shopping around for confessors who are not so desperate about the rules of thumb. The lonely and timid are our best customers, since they can only dream of sex, and we are not so violent in our attacks on impure thoughts. This is not to say that we are not kind or patient. Most priests are at their best in the confessional, and seldom do they lose their patience or compassion. But they can allow no recourse, no court of appeal. The sexual struggle is cut and dried.

There is little difference in the treatment of a child of fourteen and a young adult of twenty-five approaching marriage. We only grant that the adult has more reason to be flirting with the dangers of sin. But sexual arousal is as forbidden to the engaged as it is to the adolescents. All that is permitted anyone before marriage is the "Frenchless" kiss and the gentle embrace. Engaged couples are expected to appear at the altar as sexual strangers and the same night to share a king-size bed.

We are opposed to long courtships, so any violators who are not planning marriage within a reasonably short time are asked to break up, or to stop dating for a specific time. The Catholic soon finds out that he has a better chance of escaping confessional agony if the escapades are somewhat promiscuous than if concentrated in one relationship. College students come and tell us of the girl friend who fills the whole of their social life. It is a social life without funds that grows on discussion and deep affection. They have no immediate intention of marriage, nor have they the money or the desire to play the field. Each new girl means a series of expensive dates. She has to be charmed before she will consent to friendly economy. Or, if money is not the social problem, then shyness is. It takes some boys three or four months to get up enough nerve to meet a girl. Yet we demand that a relationship end as soon as sex emerges.[3]

Our ideal is impossible. While asking two people never to know anything but gentle affection before marriage, it asks them not to marry too young, not to extend the dating period for a prolonged time; also to get to know a great number of possible mates, and to receive the sacraments frequently. What our ideal achieves is one huge round of anxiety. Confession ends with great sincerity and noble promises. Then a weekend comes, a passionate exchange, followed by another encounter with a priest who cross-examines the roots of the relationship. The ultimatum of give up the girl or give up God often makes little sense, because God has become close for the first time in years through the prism of the relationship. The young lover is asked to abandon the only person who can make God seem real. The priest does not enjoy his task; it tears at his mercy and manhood. He, too, is without recourse, and the weight of campus sex weighs heavily on his shoulders. More than once many of us have been tearfully accused of destroying a friendship. At other times we sit for hours with sullen couples who will not abandon the sacraments, but cannot sacrifice each other's friendship.

Somehow, ironically, such an approach to sex plays into the hands of a world that makes of sex the very pulse of life. The Catholic couple, warned so frequently of the tree of good and evil, often expects of sex far more than it can give. The exchange of vows transforms a courtship of sexual sins into a paradise of sacred delights. It is a shock to learn that what watered the mouth from its distant tree was only an apple after all, and not the ambrosial honey that banished human hunger.

Unwittingly, too, the Catholic mystique of sex pushes teenagers into marriage. Since the experience of sex is guarded by solemn law, the tortured couple has to choose between the agony of a sin-ridden courtship and the confusion of a premature marriage. And the confesser is in no position to balance the "sins" of adolescence against the crime of a youthful marriage. The blind emphasis on the sin of sex clouds the future horror of a marriage without love, of children without parents.

Some go away sad, some go away angry. Some do not go away; they submit and break off a friendship with tears and prayers. Some even thank us for the courage that we give. Most, however, shake their heads, and wonder how long they can last. It is only lately that they have rebelled, only of late that they have begun to talk back in confession or to ignore it entirely. In the past we could silence doctor and teen-ager alike with the firm and gentle stroke of our decision. Now they begin to talk back, and I for one am glad.

The young do not wish to ignore our directions for dating and courtship. They would even welcome them. The directions, however, must be those of one who is guiding a personal conscience, and not the decisions of one who has absorbed it.[4] They will not submit their romance to a slide rule, nor will they measure their kisses and touches with the impersonal theorems of a moralist. We can talk to them of goals and they will listen far into the night. When we speak to them of codified specifics, however, they tell us to mind our own business. We will be their servants again when we offer them the essential freedom to learn by their mistakes, when we help them to learn a moral law which measures guilt by the hurt done to other people and not by the crisply mathematical violation of an unequivocal law.

Our legalistic approach was not always a failure. Some had the capacity to see the wisdom that lurked beneath its law. They were not troubled by the narrowness of the rules, or they entered a marriage soon enough, or after a brief enough courtship, to avoid much of the problem. Some were able to channel the sacrifice into the dynamic of their friendship, some found it a protection from close encounter, some were just too afraid to deviate. There were those, unquestionably, who approached marriage in the innocence of childhood. But even though they were the marginal few, somehow they became the norm of universal behavior. Each of us can point to a parent, a friend, even, perhaps, a spouse, who lived the Church's law of courtship to the letter and yet was not marked by hostility, confusion, or pharisaic pride. These are the exceptional people who can maintain their balance in any system. But we do not raise our children in log cabins because Lincoln seemed to prosper there.

Man also was more tolerant of such a system in another world because he did not know so much about the dynamics of courtship. We have come to realize that sex can mean a thousand different things to a thousand different people. It can mean anything from the first experience of a man's tenderness to a complete rejection of the responsibilities of love. It can mean a selfish attempt to prove something, or a genuine expression of love. But while man has acquired this new knowledge about the dynamics of courtship, the Church does not honor it.

It is an impossible procedure to listen to a voice in a dark confessional say: "I let my boy friend go too far three times," and to attempt to understand what is involved in sin and psychology. There is no time or method to discover what sex means to this person, no chance to discuss the fear of being "an old maid" that frightens this girl as much as the fear of hell. "If he *really* loves you, he can be pure," we say, and our calm decision requires no evidence or justification. We say it so often we are certain of it. We can never ask: "What do you think? Does it seem wrong? Is this sincere friendship, or a fear of growth and communication?" We know the answer before we ask. It is impurity and impurity is irresponsible love.

But we cannot blame the priest too much, for, as I have said, he suffers in his role of judge without recourse. He has learned a morality of the "individual action," a morality which numbers and categorizes mortal sin. He cannot be satisfied with "general progress" or a "growing awareness"; he must know each sin and then receive the assurance that it will not recur.

The Church must replace its blind, arbitrary formulas with an intense awareness that each man must stumble to find his way in love. It must ask more questions than it answers. It must shift the responsibility from the unyielding decision of the priest to the individual conscience that is carving out a life. To build such a religion—and the theological ground is already laid [5]—means that men have to be trusted with the right of personal decision.

Perhaps the adolescent will need more pointed directions, but even he will know new freedom to make mistakes, and will not fear the independence of moral judgment that must attend age and experience. I have often wondered what would indeed result if we converted the massive efforts of our dating code into a vast educational program of self-knowledge and the dynamics of personal, responsible love. It is unfortunate that we have armed our charges with such precise distinctions in matters of sex, and have spoken to them so little of the nature of friendship. Perhaps we did not know about the love of friendship ourselves.

When I speak of a program of morality that rests the sexual decisions of dating on the responsibility of a personal conscience, I can anticipate the screams of a "morality without absolutes." I know, however, that absolutes live in books and scholars' heads, whereas life is a struggle of doubt amid certitude, shadow dotted with light. If a man tells me that he sees no harm in intercourse before marriage, I can question his emotional awareness, or even his sincerity. But I can be concerned with his decision only to the degree that he lets me be. And even then we search in dialogue; I cannot preach to him in absolutes I do not understand. Man is not absolute, either in mind or heart, nor can he possess or reveal all of himself in a single act or decision. His moral attitudes may change as he himself grows and changes, but my conscience must never speak for his. Direction, yes; dictation, never.

There will always be the simple and the fearful who will ask the church to make all judgments for them. They will need the more directive help of "Father's own opinion." Life for them must be clearly laid out, and each decision must not tremble with equivocation. The increasing multitude of men, however, must hear the responsibility of their own judgments. The community with its suggestions and its alternate opinions will be the constant test of their sincerity, the god that teaches them of love and pride.

Would not marriages be much the same if we only offered general advice and permitted the individual to follow the directives of his own conscience? Could we not, for example, reexamine the goals of Christian marriage and courtship? Could we not talk to him about the dangers of false love, the obstacles to communication, the seriousness of false commitment? Could we not beg him never to rest in stagnant assurance of moral rectitude, but to continue to evaluate and grow? Cannot the true sin of sex be the consciously selfish seduction which makes of man an object and not a person? What harm has the sincere man done who made love to a fiancée with whom he will sleep for forty years of marriage? Can people not be taught to measure the rights of sexual expression by the nature of the commitment? Do they not do this already in high school, in college, in the world of factory and office? Would man not mature if we offered him a plan of growth in love and not a judicial ultimatum? Could we not say "I think" or "it seems," rather than "you must" or "you can't"? Can we not learn from married couples about what happens during courtship and what actually hurts or helps a relationship?

I know from personal experience of dozens of couples whose marriage is as successful as their courtship was passionate. Did they sin so gravely in their preparation for the marriage which ultimately gave to past sex its present meaning? If a married couple can delay the birth of children for personal reasons and yet know the enjoyment of sex, is it wrong for honestly engaged couples to communicate in a similar way? If it is wrong, why? If a love affair, not leading to marriage, teaches a man about himself, teaches him consideration and confidence, helps him to be honest and to feel warmth and pity, is it a sinful affair or an essential step in his search for the capacity to love maturely? And of what value is the conscience wrangle that goes on in Catholic courtships? [6] Is the ordinary woman, flushed with her diamond, capable of denying sex to the man who will father her children? Is the sexual abstinence required in Catholic courtship not often the club which a woman refuses to relinquish in her lifelong struggle with her man for supremacy? Is not such abstinence as blinding as sexual indulgence? Cannot the one be as dangerous a cover for fear of sex or latent homosexuality as the other can be an indication of egotism and selfishness? Is it morally good to do the right thing for the wrong reasons?

These are questions which I cannot completely answer. But they are honest questions, real questions, and they cannot be ignored with simple conclusions of an unyielding law. Man the complicated cannot be dismissed with a quiet shrug and a nod in the direction of tradition. As anthropology grows, as man's view of himself is altered, he will continue to ask new and harder questions in practical theology. If we cannot answer them, we must not tell him that we can. Love is not afraid of discipline, it thrives on it, it learns to respect it even as it grows. It is, however, as unique in each case as the two people that make up the custom-made union. We in the Church do not have a corner on concern for happy marriages. We are not alone in our search for the meaning of morality in courtship. It troubles every parent, each church and school, it troubles society itself. Most of all, it concerns the maturing couple who have some awareness of what a lifelong commitment means.

The sexual morality of the Church was unquestionably right in seeking the marital union as its point of reference. Few would quarrel with that. Sex finds its meaning and fulfillment in the marital union. But why does sin have to be measured by the presence or absence of this or that act of pleasure? Since serious sin is determined, granting freedom, by the harm done, does not an honest theology have to point out the nature of this harm? What actual harm is done when two people, who think they are in love—and who would tell them certainly they are not—express their affection in the physical dimension? Whom did they hurt by this passionate exchange? God? One another? Society? A future child? If so, how? Is it the risk of pregnancy that makes it wrong? What if there is no risk? The traditional moralist would say that only the married have a right to sexual pleasure and this would end the discussion. Or he would point to the scriptural condemnation of "fornication" without deciding whether Scripture referred to promiscuous lovemaking or preparation for marriage, whether it was describing a single action or a way of life.

What if sexual experience were a necessary way of distinguishing between infatuation and serious love? Would it then be virtuous? If a courtship leads to a happy marriage, regardless of the sexual exchange, it is not a sound courtship? Is it not, in retrospect, a holy courtship since it produced sincere human commitment? Can a courtship, no matter how "pure" and undefiled, be called "good" if it led to divorce? Does a moral theologian have no obligation to examine his presuppositions about the virtue of premarital purity if there is positive evidence that many a courtship was both "pure" and ineffective?

We have not talked much about such matters in theological circles. We have little time to draw any support from the way in which most couples conduct their courtship. Is this not important? Can we call the conduct of society merely the influence of pagan amorality? Or could it also be the growing maturity of a society which has lost its Victorian obsession with the horror of the flesh? Have other religious groups, which have offered only general directives about premarital sex, failed to produce happy and holy homes? Perhaps they did not have enough of a hold on their members to offer such a program. But perhaps, too, they believed more in the individual and refused to involve themselves in the intimacy of private love. It may well be that we have not trusted man enough, that we do not recognize that God speaks to him in channels that stem from creation and not from allegiance to the Church. Each man is human before he is Christian. Will not God offer private revelations to every man He has made if the channels are not frozen by a system? Are we afraid to believe in man, to know that he wants a happy marriage far more than he wants an exciting Saturday night? Must we bind him with absolutes that deny circumstances and experience? Is there anything truly absolute short of God Himself? Even Christ could not carry the burden of the Godhead without shadows. Can the laws enacted in His name do more?

No man can say to the morally responsible person: "You cannot receive the Church's sacrament. You have offended God seriously." This is a decision a man has to make for himself. I have found, in retreat and counseling experience, that man is far harder on himself than an objective law could be. If given a chance, man will evaluate his courtship in terms of the person with whom he seeks love. He will center his attention on goals and meaning, not on a single action or a personal "state of grace." This takes a great deal more reflection and sincerity than any effort to "avoid the occasions of sin" or to limit the good-night embrace.

Such an approach to conscience means that you must believe in man. You must respect his right to make personal decisions and you must realize that he wants personal happiness with divinely sparked intensity. Is this a Protestant morality? A Jewish morality? A humanistic morality? I am not sure if any group offers the proper balance of personal freedom and well-defined goals. I only know what I try to offer is the personal understanding of Christian morality that study, experience, and prayer have offered me. It is the freedom of the sons of God, the opportunity to make of a systematic creed a personal faith. No system can ever absorb man, it can only serve and direct him in his search for honest commitment. Some will be certain that sex before marriage is wrong. Others will insist that it is noble and essential. Neither group must be barred from the sacraments in the name of some absolute that makes men the docile slaves of a system.

To learn a trade or to absorb an education is a series of successes and mistakes. It cannot be measured by income or scholastic records. To learn to love is a lifetime task; it cannot be measured by "purity" or "the keeping of the law." There is only one law, the Christian law of love, and no love affair of man and man, or man and God, can ever be the same. One woman asks of a man kindness in the name of love. Another loves him for his sensitive pride. Yet another loves a loud and boisterous man, while this one wants him quiet and pensive. One man goes to love with a volcano of locked hostility, another with a deep fear that he cannot be loved. One is passionate and impulsive, another talkative and philosophic, this one is shy and inhibited. Yet each must know love if he is to know God. Each will love another human being, and God Himself, in a unique and personal way. Who is to say which act will bring love, and which will tear a man from the core of himself and his God?

Love must ever be a quest, an experiment. It must have

bounds, but only bounds that are broad enough to permit breath. Most of all, it must have freedom or it will die. In all my efforts as a priest, the purest girl I ever knew was a Mexican Negro who lived in the heart of the slums. Her mother was an alcoholic, her father perpetually unemployed. She was a beautiful girl, twenty years old, and of exceptional olive complexion. She was working part time to buy food for the family, attending college at night, and attempting a moderate social life. I gave her private instructions and got to know her well. She told me of her childhood, of the free exposure to sex, of the virginity that she had guarded for the man she would one day love. She came to the Church in innocence, and lived a life of purity before she heard mention of our rules. She knew nothing of our multiple laws, nothing of the harassing provided the Catholic conscience. She was baptized with tearful eyes, she received communion with joy she could not contain. She was open, honest, loving, pure. Somehow she found her purity with God in the slums—and she knew nothing of our rules.

9.   CHRISTIAN MARRIAGE

AND DIVORCE

It is hard to hide the scars of an unhappy marriage. They are visible when the smile fades, when a sudden burst of sadness hits in the midst of a crowded room. The unhappily married have a way of draining the meaning out of a remark that was not meant to be profound. They question you, explore your mind with too searching an intent, change your relaxed grin into a serious and wrinkled look. They want answers, and the time or place is not of great concern. That's why I was not surprised when—why don't we call her Jean—asked me if I had a few minutes to talk after a Parent-Teachers meeting one evening. We walked from the auditorium to the rectory and before we reached my office, she had started to cry.

She apologized and told me that she had not been sleeping well. I told her not to mind her tears, offered her a box of Kleenex, and she lit up a cigarette. She and her doctor husband had been married for seventeen years. They had two boys, Dick, fifteen, and John, thirteen, both adopted. I knew the boys well, since they stayed around the gym a lot, and each responded vigorously to my least show of interest. She told me how much they thought of me and I knew she was struggling to get to her story.

She had met her husband, Don, when he was an intern at

a local hospital. Don was from a broken home, his father having disappeared when Don was in eighth grade. Jean had never felt close to Don's mother, but they lived far enough away so that she seemed no problem. They had visited her only twice during their courtship, and somehow she wasn't able to attend the wedding, which took place in Jean's parish. It was only two months later that she discovered Don was a homosexual.

I asked if he had given evidence of this during the courtship. She answered with a touch of bitterness that she had felt he was just being a good Catholic when he never got "carried away." After marriage they had had intercourse only twice, both times on their eight-day honeymoon. For a time Jean had been able to show Don affection, but after a few weeks he would move away whenever she touched him. For seventeen years Jean had never made love. He had brought his friends home in odd assortments, until she had "put her foot down" when she discovered him with one of his friends making love on the living-room floor. She said that she had prayed to forgive him, but never could. She had gone to the parish priest and he had listened with sympathy. He suggested that they adopt children and Jean had agreed that only this could give any meaning to her life. And while the two boys had not dulled the pain, they had given her a reason to go on.

Lately, it seemed, there was no reason to continue. The boys didn't need her as much, she was beginning to drink, she found it difficult to sleep. She had tried the hospital auxiliary, the Junior League, programs to establish mental health, to help the Negro, to provide entertainment for the aged. But none seemed to help, and presently she found herself longing to be held in the arms of a man who cared. She converted trifles into complicated fantasies. The touch of a postman's hand, a social dance with one of her husband's friends, even a glance from an attractive man—each set her flesh trembling and her mind echoing with confusion. She had never been unfaithful, she was not sure that she could be.

She found herself staring in the mirror, watching each new

wrinkle give emphasis to the one before. Every pound she gained seemed to speak of loneliness and death. Her figure had become almost the measure of her worth. Of late she was on the verge of tears every time her husband was obliged to take her out socially among associates. She was the female that accompanied him, the hired wife that gave him acceptability among his peers, the middle-aged woman who had never known the needs of a man. Her husband worked endless hours to amass money. They lived in a hundred-thousand-dollar home, each drove a new Cadillac, had twice as many clothes as anyone could want. But she would throw it all away to know a husband's love.

The boys, she told me, had never really had a father. They looked for substitutes and hung on every new priest or teacher that came into their lives. At that moment, the basketball coach and I were the constant subject of their conversation. Don had never spent time with them, and she was just as glad because she feared the company he kept. She had played ball with the boys, cheered at the little league games, praised and corrected them. Five years ago she had talked to a Jesuit who was giving a conference in the parish. He seemed to have the kind of heart that would understand and the kind of mind that would know some special court of recourse. He had studied in Rome and the resonant confidence of his voice gave her some new and strange hope. He had listened, and when she had finished the outline of her story, he only shook his head. He was moist around the eyes and his voice was not as resonant as before. He had nothing new to say, but he promised to write her. He signed his letters "With love," and for a time this was indeed her secret love. Of late, however, the letters were occasional, and the melody of his words had lost their impact. He spoke of suffering with the clear distinctions of a man who had never known its awesome power to torture memories and transform ideals. She was losing the language of the Christian dream, and words like "Cross" and "saint" no longer rang with the mystery of childhood.

The sacraments, once her contact with sanity, had become

empty forms, the sermons in church seemed the pious sentiments of untried boys. Only her sons were real, their hair damp with sweat, their appetites eager for fun and food. Only her sons gave her life and the thought of them kept the sleeping pills bottled in the medicine cabinet. Her inflection underplayed the drama of her words, and after forty minutes she had said it all. I had no questions, and all the answers I had were forbidden by my Church.

This was a marriage in Christ, the law insisted, since it fulfilled all the prescribed patterns. Two baptized Catholics had been married by a priest. The marriage had been consummated—granted, only twice in seventeen years—and now it was sealed in the iron ledger of some eternal apocalypse. They were "two in one flesh," the manuals said, bound in the mysterious intimacy of Christ and His Church. The nuptial blessing had warned her to be "faithful to one embrace," "to flee unlawful companionship," to emulate the faith of Sara, Rachel, and Rebecca. She was the valiant woman who knew that beauty was vain and fleeting, who watched it fade each morning and wept for it each night. She had been told by Paul himself to "obey" her husband since she would be cherished as his own flesh. Time had told her that she could not love her husband, despite Paul or Pope or Christ Himself. She could only stay with him in barren union, afraid to leave him only because she feared to lose her God.

Jean was not alone in the limping procession of married martyrs that came to me for answers when I could give them only a memorized text. There were hundreds more! There was Harry, who married Sharon at eighteen, when sex seemed to contain all that love promised. She had left him after two years, left him and the house and the baby as well. She had married again and gave him the child to care for in his Catholic celibacy. I had talked with her, pleaded with her, but the iron of her eyes had told me that she no longer listened to the Church. One kiss from her new-found man would blot out a thousand words from priestly lips. Harry was alone for almost four years, and then he married again in love and need. His parents would not attend the wedding or purchase a gift. They cut him off with all the courage of a canonical theology that knows no exceptions. He was not welcome in his father's house; his mother could kiss her granddaughter before her son's remarriage, and after close the door. Harry was excommunicated from the Church and ripped from the family that had raised him. He had protested that his marriage to Sharon was the decision of a boy, and the pressures of an unhappy home had pushed him into a premature union. Harry could protest, but no one listened. He heard the whispers of the Catholic community until the fury of the ghetto morality drove him to another town.

The litany I remember is endless: the spouses who watched a home disintegrate around an alcoholic, the teen-agers who thought marriage meant only freedom to make love in their own apartment. It includes the man married to a helpless psychotic, the woman bound to an angry beast, the couple who have not spoken a direct and personal word in twenty years. It embraces the nervous little ladies who make novenas for their husbands to abandon the barmaids or wait for their men to get out of jail and make them pregnant. There are sadists and masochists, beaters and brawlers, profane and rigid dictators who match Hitler at his worst. Yet the law says these men and women are united in Christ and that no power on earth can loose the bond. They are to choose between the distant hope of a miraculous reform or the lonely life of parents without partners. And while they debate the decision of divorce, they stay together long enough to have another child, to incur another time payment, to suffer another breakdown, to grow too old to care. If they finally leave their private hell, they are told never to date, never to kiss, never to linger near the "occasion of sin," and, ultimately, never to love.

And in all this fierce legalism, what does my Church propose to gain? It says that marriage is the human image of Christ's relationship with the Church. It says that every couple who are married in the Church are united in Christian love. The husband must cherish his wife as his own body, and she must treat him as her very blood and heart. The children must feel the overflowing warmth of this union and grow strong and secure in the patience and kindness that pervade the home. There will be quarrels, but forgiveness must be sought before the day is at an end. There will be sickness, a retarded child, financial pressures, a sense of failure that plagues the middle years. There will be trouble in school, fights at the dinner table, flareups and sullenness, jealousies and sleepless nights. But husband and wife must bear the burden of the day and seek to nourish love in the prayer and silence of the night.

Such an ideal cannot be questioned, and any Church does well to promulgate such hopes. I have seen such marriages in every parish that I served. I remember the tall businessman and his redhaired wife, and the houseful of children that welcomed my frequent calls. The husband's pride showed whenever his wife told an anecdote about the children, or when she insisted I eat a sandwich and drink a beer. She kidded him and he loved it, with even the children joining the good-natured banter. It was a happy home, the best of Christian homes, where love and interest lived in every room. The children were bright, enthusiastic, each with a dozen hobbies, each with a unique and obvious place in the parents' hearts. Jimmy was retarded, but in his bubbling joy for life, he didn't seem to know it or to mind. Ellen planned to be a nun, and her love for practical jokes could spark any community to whom she gave her vows. Dave could think of nothing but football in the fall, pestered me to throw him passes, and to show him how to block. There were dogs in the yard, rabbits in the garage, and snakes and guinea pigs in the basement. The house was a menagerie, a circus, a dormitory, a subway station, a sanctuary —a home. Here were parents, here were children, here was love!

Every home could not know such happiness, some could only remember it from years gone by. I remember the gray-haired father of fifty-five who called and told me he needed my help. I had known and admired him for several years. I had taught his children in high school and chatted with him and his wife at every parish function. But his call sounded like trouble, so I went as quickly as I could. He met me at the door and stopped me at the porch. He wanted to prepare me for the problem, to explain his alcoholic wife. He was embarrassed, confused, unable to tell me coherently what had happened in his home. She had just begun to drink excessively a few months ago. She had drunk socially and moderately for years, but suddenly had lost control. Her anger was violent, her language coarse and snarled, her tantrums made the younger children cry.

It was a miserable visit that only prefaced others twice again as bad. I don't know how he stood it, but he loved her and remembered the gentle days gone by. At times, as she lay in a drunken stupor and ceased her screaming for a time, he recalled their vacations, their fun with the children, the card games with friends, the closeness and confidence they shared. I listened to his stories, laughed at the funny things she'd done, and watched a man in love struggle to keep his sanity, his hope, his marriage. There was no talk of divorce; she needed him, he loved her, and that was all there was to say. But he needed me and the comforts of the Church. I prayed with him, watched him come more regularly to Mass, gave him the assurance that this crisis would pass. And it did.

This, too, was a permanent marriage; this, too, was an obvious union in Christ. It was not as carefree as the home of the businessman and his redhaired wife. But it was Christian. It was an enduring bond that held a suffering man to his alcoholic wife. It was not my Church that kept him at her side. It was not his vows, his children, his honor, his pride that held him faithful; it was his love. He loved her because he loved her in the sacrament of love. He was not a sullen martyr who fought to honor a promise made in youth. He did not want to hear of his nobility, his patience, his Christian fortitude. It was not the fear of hell that frightened him to save a marriage, but the love for his wife that offered him no other course.

This is marriage; this is the answer to easy and impulsive divorce. But what of the twenty-year-old girl who came barefoot in her robe to the rectory door one cold November night? She sobbed convulsively on the steps. Her face was swollen and bloody, her right eye was completely closed. I knew her and the angry boy she had married, who threatened her with death. She would not go back to him, she screamed for the baby that lay in a crib while a mad young man was raging through the house. I asked her what had happened, but she wouldn't answer until I called the police and brought the baby to her side. She told me that he had returned from a poker game and asked her for a cigarette. She didn't have one, and he demanded that she go out and get some. She refused and he began to beat her until she thought he would kill her on the spot. Now she was in my office. She held the baby close and the policeman drove her to her parents' home. What of her?

She was married in my Church. She exchanged her vows before her God. She knelt at the altar, received communion with her husband, and heard the priest describe the beauty that is married love. Her hopes were high, her resolutions intent, her love was young, but serious and strong. Three months later she was living in hell. He lost his job and refused to work. She supported him while he played basketball and drank. He slapped her, abused her, brought home lipstick on the shirts she washed. He didn't pray or go to Church, or speak a decent word. And when the baby arrived, he was only annoyed. But he was a Catholic, and so was she, and the priest had married them in Church. This, therefore, was an endless union in Christ, she only had to wait and try until she knew the joy of Holy Mary or the peace of St. Theresa. Or she could offer her suffering for the souls in purgatory and wait for the heaven promised to the patient miserable who do not kill themselves. She was married forever, and there was nothing more to tell her in my Church.

The Pope did not have to tell her this as he talked to diplomats or begged for world peace. I had to tell her. The Pope was worried about Vietnam, or nuclear war, or the Irish bishops who balked at reform. I was worried about her, and I carried her sorrow as I preached on Sunday or taught the teen-agers about marriage. My bishop did not have to tell her as he worried about collections or hurried to confirm the docile children who nervously kissed his ring. My bishop did not take her to the Council, or explain her marriage to the theologians, or see her crumpled on the steps in the middle of the night. He told me to tell her that she had been joined in Jesus Christ, that she could not stop and start again. So I told her, like a coward, like an obedient Catholic priest, who could violate his conscience in fealty to his Church.

It was not only this little one I told. I told the lawyer who came to me by night. I heard him describe his marriage as a lasting cold war. There were no blows, no violent explosions, only ugliness and hate. His wife was a social climber who enjoyed each new and more expensive house until there were no more guests to impress, no more articles on the society page describing the parties held in her elegant mansion. She dragged him to parties he couldn't stand, pushed him to entertainment that depressed him, and brought him back to a home where he led a sexless life. Her taste in clothes and homes kept him working dangerous hours, and yet he was endlessly in debt. He liked simple things like conversation and an occasional outing with the children. He liked to read, to walk, to associate with friends who offered more than money and prestige.

He had conceded to her tastes for a time, hoping he could recapture the friendship that courtship had seemed to promise. At other times he had fought her, demanded that she be his wife, told her that nothing satisfied her and nothing short of an honest marriage ever could. She turned her back, lost herself in bridge and art, added more important people to her list. Finally, he had given up. Any suggestion he made was ridiculed, any effort he made was never quite enough. Suddenly he could take it no longer. He was tired of cajoling her, of indulging her, of living as a stranger in his house. There were no family meals, no laughs or simple fun. He loved his children but they were not enough. He could not bear to leave them, but he was only pushing them away in the bitterness of his marriage and hurting them in his hatred for his wife. He had tried everything. He had prayed, sought guidance from a counselor, even tried to make friends with the people who spoke artificially of opera and art. Now it was over; he had tried enough to make a marriage of a contract that only brought him misery and debt. He asked for an answer, and I gave him the party line. He asked for understanding, and I had nothing more to say. I could only make him feel guilty about leaving the children, or suggest that he was intolerant and rude.

So he went away, divorced her, and left the Church. Was this the marriage of which Paul in his epistle speaks, where wives are subject to their husbands and husbands love their wives? Or was this only hatred, only game-playing, self-destruction, and horror? But my Church had spoken, changing water into wine, by calling misery "marriage" and hatred "home." Nothing could permit him to leave his wife and try again. There was no hope, no excuse, no second chance, and with such a conclusion my Church had done its job. The Pope could sleep, my bishop could sip his wine and eat his evening meal. I could cry or curse or get busy and try to forget. But the Catholic man, the lawyer, the father, could only linger in his guilt.

And on Sunday, when he comes to Mass, we'll talk about divorce. We tell him that secularism, neopaganism, and hedonism have increased the incidence of divorce. We tell him that we are the valiant moral guardians in the garbage pile of civilization. We blame Hollywood, which has made light of marriage in its lives and its movies. But its lives evoke men's pity, not their imitation, and its movies only reflect the tensions in modern life. We blame freedom of the sexes, the modern fashions which seem to offend bishops, the early dating pattern of our youth. But every generation has had a scapegoat for its own weakness, and has blamed the young for what their elders taught them. We blame the laws that make divorce easy, and the lawyers and counselors who urge it on their clients. But we do not realize that divorce is never easy, save in the minds of the celibates, who do not understand what the loss of children, the legal wranglings, and alimony mean. We forget that divorce requires the great courage to face loneliness, society's disdain, parents' wrath, friends' criticism, and children's tears. We do not tell our people that divorce can be a martyr's way and the way of loveless marriage a concession to convenience.

We speak of divorce in the simple categories of defensive minds which have never loved. We do not recognize that divorce is a deep wound among the weak and ordinary men, an abiding sense of failure, a lost vocation, a shattered dream, a growing guilt, a secret fear that one may not be capable of giving or winning love. It well may be a relief, but it is seldom simple. And so, steeped in our callowness and inexperience, our smugness and ignorance, we condemn divorce and blame it on everyone but ourselves.

Why do we not blame it on the dullness of our religion, on a structure grown sterile and foreign, on sermons that didn't say anything relevant, on a Christ Who has been made as mute as steel and ice? Why not blame it on a theology that condemned adultery with eloquence, but couldn't say anything important about love? We spend time priding ourselves on the strength of our many-babied homes, but do not hear the groans of the babies grown to manhood. We are satisfied to call self-fulfillment "selfishness" and to rant with dishonest conservatives about a society saturated with sex, bikinis, and dashing Bond men. It does no good to rant of this, to condemn it, to threaten mothers with the premature pregnancy of their daughters. We need interpreters, not angry orators who lack the wisdom and experience to match their words.

Man wants interpreters, and is weary of our scolding and our misplaced blame. He does not want divorce, he merely accepts it when there is no other course. He is not concerned about the fearful statistics, he is concerned about himself. He wants to love, not to know the reasons why the selfish world never can. And what help have we given him? Has my Church encouraged him to be emotionally honest, or has it helped to bury his emotions in anger and fear? Has it given him a personal God, urged him to discover this God in the loving closeness of another human being, or has it only demanded that he keep the rules? Has it told him of the need for maturity and offered him a possible way of finding it, or has it only been rigid in its rules on sex and often forced him into a legal contract to quiet his scrupulous conscience? My Church can blame no one for divorce unless it as vigorously blames itself.

It has taught man less than psychology about love, less than group therapy, less than quiet discussions that bring men to bars and coffeehouses, less than the movies or TV. It has taught men rules, discipline, and endurance. It has not taught men friendship, marriage, love.

If my Church permitted divorce, it fears, every home would be threatened. This is an exaggeration. Catholics are not struggling to save a marriage simply because the Church threatens them with excommunication if they marry a second time. The divorce rate among Catholics is not lower than that among other honest men. Divorce is more often a reflection of an impossible marriage than a mirror of irreligion in the world. People stay together, with few exceptions, because they love each other, or because a broken home costs too much in personal effort, confused children, and social criticism. Only a minority are restrained by religious conviction when the chance for real love presents itself with reasonable convenience. A change in the Church's attitude toward divorce would free this miserable minority, and relieve the torturous guilt of those who have remarried without the blessing of their Church.

The Church is not keeping marriages together, people are. To say that men would lose their balance if the law governing the permanence of marriage were more humble and honest is to lose faith in man's capacity to love. Man wants to marry once, to remain married for life, to enjoy his children's children. We do not have to command this; we only have to show him how. But we cannot tell him that God demands that he live with a spouse he does not love. No honest man will listen, and only frightened men will obey.

Long enough has the legalist told us that Christ denied the possibility of divorce. No honest Scripture scholar can assert that Christ or early Christianity did more than uphold permanent marriage as the ideal, the fruit of Christian love.[1] He cannot say that a contract witnessed in the Church, any valid contract, makes a marriage as lasting as man's life. Modern Catholic theologians are more honest. They tell us that it is not the ceremony and consent that makes of marriage a permanent sacrament, but *the presence of Christian love*.[2] It is the presence of this unique love which distinguishes marriage from every other form of society. This special love gives marriage its meaning and determines whether this is a union born of God or a misfortune that should be remedied. Society's other forms, such as clubs or even fraternities, can well endure without personal love, but marriage is unique. Love is not merely one of its aims, but its very center and core. The man who cannot love cannot truly be married in Christ, no matter the sons he has fathered. He well may enter a contract that creates responsibilities, but to call this Christian marriage would make a mockery of the vision of Christ.

The canon law of my Church does not even mention married love in its description of the purposes of marriage. This is proper enough, since love is not a purpose of marriage but its creative cause. Even the children cannot move the husband from the center of his wife's heart, or the unique union of marriage is in jeopardy. Love for children must somehow be merged in the mutual love of husband and wife. When a man falls in love, he has found his other self, he has found the chance for fullness offered by the God Who made him empty. He will not be replaced in his beloved's heart by children or relatives, by the amusing or the profound, or even by his Church. It is the union of love which speaks to him of God. If you call him proud and selfish to search for such love, you condemn the Creator Who fashioned man in the very image of His jealous love.

The law does not deal with such mysteries. It mentions the purposes of marriage: the procreation of children, mutual help, and the calming of passion. Love, however, is the essence of marriage, even as love is the essence of Christianity, or any honest faith. Christ gave special meaning to marriage that this peak of human love might more clearly resemble His own.

Where there is not love, there is no sacrament, no Christian marriage. This does not even mean that the sacrament endures if once there was love. The contract endures until the rights of each party have been protected, until the children are provided for, but the permanent sacrament ceases when love is at an end. The legalist in my Church can call a hate-filled union a Christian sacrament of marriage; the honest theologian never can, he never should.

There is nothing to prevent my Church from declaring null any union which has lost its substance, that is, any marriage which has lost its love. This does not mean that divorce should be granted with ease. Nor does it mean that the innocent can be ignored, or the rights of children overlooked. It only means that a pregnant teen-ager will not have to pay for a mistake until the end of her life. It means that a man who married for sex at twenty may long for love at thirty, and we cannot tell him he is bound in a sterile union for life. It means that Jean, married to a homosexual, will not lose her place in the Church if she remarries. It means that the lawyer who lives with a social-climbing stranger will not be bound by empty form. It does not mean that men may run from marriage at the least pressure or provocation, but it does mean that they will not have to endure a relationship that is teeming with hatred and anguish.

There is no law, of course, which can measure the existence of love in marriage. We will have to trust a man when he tells us that he has no love. We will have to take his word, as we do in confession, and not make him prove the facts he only has to state. Canonists demand proof and require witnesses, legalists smother a man with forms to fill out and oaths to swear. A Christian takes his word and leaves judgment to his conscience and his God.

Locked in the memory box of my childhood is a sad face that I knew and loved in my youth. She was a middle-aged Catholic who sold candy to a little boy in a grocery store. She was kind to me, patient with my selection of four cents' worth of sweets. She always made me feel good, told me how handsome I looked when I served at the altar in Church. She said she would have liked a son as polite as I was, and I wondered why she couldn't have one. I knew little about her and only cared, as is the way with little ones, that she was kind and interested in me. One day I heard that she had divorced and remarried, and in my childish mind our friendship was over. I still bought candy, but I was painfully strained and different. She sensed it in my unspoken words and downcast eyes. One day she touched my hair and I pulled away. She looked at me with the saddest face I can recall, and said, "Someday I hope you'll understand!"

I do not know where life has taken her. I do not even know where it has taken me. But from my heart, I say to the sad face of my youth, "I do understand; forgive me!"

10. BIRTH CONTROL

"A dozen times I practiced birth control," a Catholic man says to me in my confessional. He tells me his name that I may better understand his problem. I know his children. They are a joy to have in school, a reflection of a man and woman's love. I know he has tried "rhythm" since the night he told me that he could name each of his last three children "Our Mistake." I know he has practiced abstinence until his wife was too edgy to live with, and he was masturbating twice a week. I have talked to him again and again, I have offered him all my solutions, described the homemade remedies hatched in a celibate's mind. Once I even suggested separate beds, so ignorant was I of a man's relationship with his wife.

And now he comes again, not to the Pope, not to the bishops, but to me in the confessional, and I have nothing more to say. My training tells me that he is living in "mortal sin," that without the forgiveness of confession he could die and go to hell. I cannot tell him this. He is among the best men I know. He is responsible, talented, sensitive, generous with money and time. His eyes are clear, his private life above reproach, his friends loyal, his wife still deeply in love, his children happy and full of life. But my Church accuses him and forbids him to receive communion until I take away his "sins." Tomorrow, first-communion Sunday for his seven-year-old boy, he cannot join his family at the table of Christ unless he is free from mortal sin. So I forgive him again with kindness and wait a month to forgive him yet again.

He goes back home to watch the children and to give his wife her chance to confess. She summons up her courage, holds back her tears, enters the confessional, whispers her guilt, and waits for the sermon that will make her feel dirty and ashamed. She takes me into the bedroom, tries to tell me what marriage is like, tries to explain the needs of her husband and her own desire for warmth. She recalls the calendar she threw away, the thermometer that lied to her about her ovulation, the confusion of charts and graphs and organized love. There are supposed to be several days a month, when intercourse might possibly be "safe." Yet she is not sure, and when these days come around, she is so tense that she fails at lovemaking. She ends up weeping and hoping her husband will somehow understand.

Lately she has noticed that he has grown a little cool. His expression has changed, he is drinking more. She herself has been increasingly nervous. If he puts his arm around her when he is watching TV, she fears he will lead her into sin. If he kisses her firmly on his return from work, she can feel her shoulders pull away. She tells me she is growing bitter and has lost much feeling for her Church. She asks permission to take the pill and wonders what I think. I hesitate. I know she will tell her friends what I said, if only to quiet her conscience, which has so long depended on the Pope. If I tell her to use the pill, then I will be swamped by the guilty who will ask to join my exodus. If I say "no," I will trample on my own conscience and send a sinner back to sin again. So I do not answer. I forgive her in the name of Jesus and leave her as wounded as before.

I do not answer because I do not agree with my Church, and I am hardly prepared to let my bishop tear the priesthood from my back. If I preach the conclusions I have reached by reflection and experience, I will be condemned to silence. If I forgive the couple who live in misery and suggest they use the pill, my rights to hear confessions will be revoked. So I turn to my fellow priests and ask for wisdom. The young are almost unanimous in their refusal to believe the Church, but they are too frightened to stand alone. The old tell me of their own dear mother who raised a family of ten, and boast of the happiness they enjoyed in their father's house.

These older men, vigorous in their opinions and usually Irish in background, deserve a special place in the annals of my Church. For years they prevented me from forming my own opinions, so strong were their sentiments, so firm their voices, so white and dignified their hair. I did not see the deep resentment in their blood, which somehow merged Margaret Sanger with the English Crown. I only saw the courage in their eyes and heard the lilt of deference when they greeted parishioners with a family full of children. They talked of Marie and her brood of ten, they extolled Louise and her six in seven years, they invited the bishop to baptize Helen's twelfth. But neither Louise nor Marie nor Helen could match their own Irish mothers, who chopped wood, kneaded dough, taught school, shoveled snow, nursed eleven babies, and attended daily Mass. All I could do was pant in the presence of such sacrifice and wonder if the world had not lost it pristine light. In the company of these priests, birth control was Communism, or Freemasonry, or the lust of Caesar's court.

No one dared question them, or ask them if they had read the modern arguments that justified the pill. They treated rhythm as a concession to weakness and urged newlyweds to let God and Mary shape the family size. They read nothing but the daily paper and the priestly journals, which confirmed their prejudices and gave fuel to their ancient arguments. They knew no theology and they dismissed fresh thought with a startled look, a puff on their pipe or cigar, and an abrupt change of subject. They were sure that nothing exciting had happened in religious thought since Christ surprised his Apostles on Easter Sunday morn. They rarely heard confessions, and when they did, the pious flocked to them, the "sinners" stayed away.

Such men are rarer now, but the power of their impact lingers in the Church. Even as I write, I think of the white-haired pastors who will hate me for my words. It is hard to hurt them, hard to oppose them in their declining years. They can point to the noble graduates of their schools, the prominent men who would not miss their Sunday sermons, the grown men and women who live only because parents listened to their priestly words on birth control. It is hard to hurt them because they are prayerful men, who read the Mass with dignity and simple, honest faith. It is hard to hurt the generation that they formed, the men and women who obeyed each sentence they uttered. These are my parents, my relatives, the loyal laity that gave me respect in the parishes I served. It is hard to hurt them, to meet their gaze, to know that I disturb the principles that have guided their whole life.

And yet it is harder to sit in my office and to hear the middle-aged doctor and his wife. He is not a Catholic, while she was trained from first grade through womanhood by nuns. She had even flirted with the convent, but recognized that marriage, too, is a dedicated love. Her husband does the talking in our conference. He speaks of six children and four miscarriages in a dozen years. His wife has spent over seven months in the hospital. They have always practiced rhythm, since her conscience would accept nothing else. Recently, she has had her fourth miscarriage and a solemn warning from her obstetrician that another pregnancy might take her life.

I wait for his question, and even as I wonder how he'll phrase it, I know the hollowness that will punctuate my words. He asks it simply: "What is wrong with birth control?" I reach in the grab bag of arguments handed me by my Church. I hear a voice that sounds like mine speak of primary purposes and natural law.[1] It says foolish things that only frightened men can hear. I hear the voice suggest abstinence or a new thermometer, or gratitude to God for all they have.

The doctor and I listen to the voice that sounds like mine, and we are not impressed. We think of six children, miscarriages, and a battered little wife. We think of the comfort she needs to care for the children she has, the recreation she needs to restore her energy and zest. We hear six children screaming for attention, we see clothes to be washed and sorted, housework to be done, food to be prepared. We do not believe that birth control is unnatural. It does not trouble the Jews and Christians, who love as much as we. Are they sinners? Pagans? Lusting and selfish men? We do not believe that sex is merely the bait to trick wives into another pregnancy, to lure husbands into feeding another mouth. We believe it is a road to tenderness, a special kind of conversation, the balm of loneliness, the sense of being needed and wanted amid rejection, the source of strength and comfort that teaches love. The doctor and I know that his wife needs his body that she may explore his soul, that he needs hers that he may penetrate the barriers to closeness, the sealed emotions, the secret sources of her pain.

He does not need her when her temperature is right. She does not need him when the calendar permits. He does not seduce her on a special evening like a man who dates a woman twice a month. She does not whisper as she kisses, "Yes, tonight!" She sleeps with him, studies him, notes the nervousness that attends his work, touches him to let him know she cares. He does not regulate his passion like a Stoic on display. Her sadness, a sick and sleeping child, evokes it. A song can send him to her bed, a special conversation, an evening of lightness and laughter, his hour of triumph or despair. The calendar can make of sex a duty and smother its spontaneity. Sex is a mystery never quite the same. It can uncover the hurts that preoccupation ignored, restore the closeness that routine and business wore away. All of this I know, as does the doctor and his wife. But we listen to the voice that sounds like mine, and hear it drone of selfishness and sin.

Suddenly the doctor stands, shakes his head, and takes his wife by the arm. It is only when he makes ready to leave that I realize the droning voice was mine. I want to tell him of my thoughts, but he does not want to hear any more. He has heard enough. He stands in the doorway and looks at me with sadness, with pity, with quiet, manly tears. He utters no protest, nor does he bombard me with biological arguments of his own. He only pauses to ask, "Have you ever loved a woman, Father, loved her enough to cry? Have you ever seen her bleed from a dead baby and wondered if she could live to mother the ones she had? Have you ever fondled her tired body, watched her breast heave as she lay asleep, and wondered how you'd live if she were gone? Have you ever held her when nothing else would do? Cried in her arms when you were afraid of life? Dried her tears when her duties drove her mad, then watched her smile?"

Now he is gone, his questions ringing in my ears. What do I tell him: "Obey the Church?" "Life is fleeting?" "You have not prayed?" Should I remind him of the suffering in Vietnam, or tell him that life is a valley of tears? Should I recite the arguments I've heard a thousand times, the arguments that nauseate me with their sordid view of sex, and amuse me with their puritan prejudice? Shall I tell the doctor about Onan in the Bible, who spilled his seed and was murdered by God? Or shall I tell him of Augustine's fourth-century views and his distorted references to sex? Or shall I recall the warnings of Pope Pius XI, the patron saint of the Church's present position, the warnings born of nineteenth-century theology and a medieval vision of man? Or maybe I should tell him that the Council Fathers are thinking of him in their annual meetings and the Pope will give an answer when all the facts are in.[2]

I told him *nothing* because there was nothing else to tell. Unless I told him that I was a coward who let my Church hide my conscience in the comfort of its skirts. Or told him that I was afraid to argue with my bishop, or place my priest's vocation on the block. Or told him I had been brainwashed in my training and was incapable of an independent thought.[3] Or maybe I should send him to Holland, where the theologians seem almost brave enough to tell the truth. Or best of all, tell him to inaugurate a rally in every diocese in our land, to make our people picket the rectories and gather on the bishops' porches, boycott schools, and deny parishes their weekly funds. Then maybe the Pope will hear in the silence of his chapel. Maybe he will not have to study so long, pray so fervently, if he finally hears the screams of men and women in the world.

I ask my Pope if he knows he is tearing homes apart, if he knows that Catholic men and women sexually grow apart. I see it every day, the frigidity caused by calendars, the anger and unfaithfulness of husbands, the anxiety and bitterness of wives. Some are strong enough finally to ignore the Pope when suffering is such that it threatens their sanity. The weak and docile, however, still count the days and run to confession when they violate our rules. They ask me when I see them on the streets: "When will the Pope tell us if we can use the pill?" "Do you think he'll permit it?"

Poor deluded children of the Pharaoh, making their bricks in Egypt without the straw that gives them strength. They come to me as Moses, or wait for the Pope to see a burning bush. I am Moses without charter, Moses without a single miracle, Moses without the guiding hand of God. I am a poor man's Moses, who has seen the foreign law which oppresses my people, and can only scream: "Let my people go!" Let wives go to their husbands and let husbands stop murdering their wives. Let my people go to the sacrament of communion when all they've done is love as human beings. Let my people go to confession without telling me what happens in their beds. Let Catholics go free from the consuming guilt that withers love.

The poor are made to play a vicious game when we bar them from the sacraments if they practice birth control. They come to Church each Sunday, but are forbidden to receive the bread which gives them life. They are in mortal sin, and everyone in Church can know. Even their children know as they stumble over their parents in the pews to approach the altar and share the food of Christ. But their parents stay behind and try to ignore the pressure from the pulpit: "Good Catholics receive communion every Sunday." They must sit there in shame, sit there separated by a pharisaic line. They are the "sinners" who live in lust and cannot share the banquet of their God.

The selfish woman can come to the altar if she begrudgingly gives her husband his bimonthly dose of sex. She has no problem with the Church's law. She loathes sex, and impassively endures it once or twice a month. But she keeps the law—not the law of love and concern, but the law of calendar and consummated sex. The sermons on birth control do not bother her, the Church's law protects her from the responsibility of tender love. She gives her husband her body to calm his physical hunger every other week, she only denies him the involvement of her heart. She does not practice birth control, she practices love control, and my Church is unconcerned. She keeps the law, controls her passion without a struggle, and smugly sits, without scruple, at the table of the Lord of Love. But the woman who loves her husband, who cannot keep the rules made by monks and celibates, must live in guilt till menopause.

One day, history will record the madness of my Church. Meanwhile, the weak and ignorant listen to the archaic arguments which support our views on birth control. They do not even sense the irony of our law. The Pope visits India, weeps for its poverty, and condemns the only sensible plan to control its teeming population. He comes to the United Nations to speak of peace and takes time for an irrelevant commercial to chastise birth control. For once he can let the world know that he can talk of peace without chewing the hand that passes out contraceptives. Instead he tells the politicians and the social workers, the diplomats and the welfare workers, even the religious leaders of the world, that they are selfish and immoral.

I might believe his concern for the warring world if he would relieve the misery of the weak and warring within his Church. We do not need his blessing, we need his openness to honest reform. He well knows how specious are our arguments against birth control, how they are merely wordy logistics which bind and frighten men. Men know nothing of the natural law;

they only know the pressure of hungry children and the tension of loveless lives. They cannot quote Augustine or Pius XI,
they can only tell the clergy how little they know about marriage and sex. They would like to ignore the Church's law, but
they cannot gamble with the fires of hell, so desperate have
we left them in their fearfulness of sin and God. Somehow our
law was broad enough to permit the nuns in the Congo to take
the pill lest they conceive the child of the savage who was
threatening to rape them. Why is it not broad enough to include the mothers of the world lest they lose the love of the
men who married them?

There is not a solid argument that prevents the Church
from permitting birth control. We only have to admit, as
every man who loves already does, that sex means something
other than conception. It is as simple as that. My Church does
not need more time to make up its mind; it only needs the
humility and courage to face facts. It does not need a special
revelation; it only needs to admit that celibates developed our
theology of marriage, and the ancestors of the rigid Irish monks
enforced it. We have become the laughingstock of the world,
the butt of a million jokes, the nineteenth-century Church in
the age of space.

Our rhythm clinics still condemn the family-planning clinics
and sincere researchers continue to study cycles and take tem-
peratures of desperate women.[4] Several days a month, all cir-
cled in red and green, admit a husband to the body of his wife.
Moods and family tensions defer to the calendar, and the creative and sensitive union of intercourse loses its human coloring
of hunger and surprise. Man, the clock-puncher, the button-
pusher, the computer-regulated, sacrifices his personal love to
cycled demands of sex without any rhythm at all. The world
watches, wonders, waits, but my arrogant Church ignores the
weak who love her and resists the necessary change.

We do not ask the Church to change her concern that husbands love wives, or its concern that children learn to know
they are unique and priceless. We realize that behind the
charts and rhythm cycles lies a Church that wants the best for

her children. That is why we can forgive the priests who invade bedrooms, the "theologians" who deny our parents their place at the communion table, even the Pope, who comes to America by air but condemns birth control as if he came with Columbus.

The home is, indeed, in jeopardy. The secular city has made us wonder where the picnic and the playground went. Fathers know that their work takes too much of their time. Mothers know that social commitments and car pools can easily exhaust them. Children feel the pressure of competition as soon as they enter school. The Church, ever a champion of the family, has a new and unprecedented job, a new chance to defend love in the nuclear age. But man does not need to hear of pills and passé problems; he needs to know the gospel that is for his peace.

I cannot see my world as lost and selfish. I cannot call the men who approve the pill the promoters of compromise, the immoral agents of crime. I can see them as the instruments of God. The pill is not nirvana, but neither is it sin. It is a help, certainly to be improved, to assist parents in co-creatorship with God. What is wrong if parents chose their children, plan their family, decide how far their love and energy can stretch? Must they guess at fertility or regulate love? Must they praise another generation, whose self-control might well have been more a product of prudery than of religious faith? Must they deny their spouse to pursue their God? I do not believe it. I do not accept my Church's stand on birth control, in conscience or in common sense.

I remember the young Mexican girl named María whose marriage I blessed some three years after she had first been married by a judge. She already had two children and I wondered how José could handle another one very soon. So I talked to María about rhythm, sensing that she knew little about calendars and charts. In the midst of explanation, she winked at me and said, "We won't have some kids for a while." Then, detecting my fear that she might be practicing sinful contraception, she grinned her special grin and said, "José says no more kids for now, *Padre*, but he still needs lots of love. So if the Church is mad, I tell her, 'You don't know José!' You see, *Padre*, I love the kids but José's the only man I got. I gotta love him, or he won't be happy and love María and the kids. And José don't look at the calendar when he makes love, but he don't want another kid right now. So . . . you know what I mean, *Padre*? That's all there is to it."

María seemed to have no dilemma. Her simple faith could solve the conscience problem built by Catholic theology. But millions are not as simple as María, millions have never learned the courage and independence born of her childlike trust in God. And somehow, tonight, after the angry arguments, and books, and papal statements, I think María has the problem resolved, and that's all there is to it.

11. CATHOLIC SCHOOLS

There is no modern folly to match that of the Catholic bishops who continue to erect Catholic schools. The Catholic school system, the pride of my youth and one of the landmarks of American history, deserves to be phased out. The Catholic school has drained the revenue of every parish, stolen the majority of religious vocations to staff its offices and classrooms, absorbed our energies and consumed our time. To sustain it we have neglected our parishes, ignored the poor, delayed renewal, and alienated our non-Catholic friends. Once upon a time such sacrifice made sense.[1]

The Catholic schools that cover our country are the valiant monuments of the zealous and weary pastors who built them to fortify their faith and the heroic people who sacrificed to pay for them. They were an emergency measure, a proof of the kind of determination that our fathers poured into our blood— the determination that would one day bring the freedom that would make these schools obsolete.

I attended such a school and I regret it not at all. I loved its old bricks and the railroad track that interrupted the classes with the hissing of its trains. I loved the sisters that taught me, and love them still. I was herded to Mass each morning and guided to confession each Friday afternoon. I did not murmur;

it was the only life I knew. It made sense to me because it made sense to my parents, and that was quite enough. I learned my religious "facts to remember" and gave a name to every sin or suggestion of the Holy Spirit. I knew that I would have to suffer for my faith, that Masons would get jobs denied to Catholics, that I was taxed for schools I didn't use. I was proud of my faith and would rather die than harm or deny it. I was convinced that I could read and spell better than my friends in the public schools, and attributed this to the special wisdom given me by God. I sold my raffle tickets with vigor, ransomed black babies from pagan lands, and had free days that my public school friends didn't share.

My school is a noble part of America's history, a witness to the accumulated bigots of Europe's religious wars. I was accused of idolatry and of orphanages filled with the babies of nuns. I was reminded of Galileo and Torquemada as if they slept with me at night. I was not alone in my suffering; I lived in a ghetto as did the Negroes and the Jews. I clung to my fellow Catholics when my countrymen called me ignorant and superstitious. My friends were the Polacks, the Dagos, the Hunkies, and the shanty Irish of America's bloody birth. I knew in my way what the Mexicans and Puerto Ricans know, what the Protestants in Spain have known, what man everywhere has known when he threatens the security and comfort of the party in power. And so my parish built my school, as Catholics throughout my country built their schools, when they were denied religious rights and self-respect. They built them with the meager income that an immigrant could make, with their own hands if there was no other way. They built them, and I, like all America, should be proud. They could do nothing else, given their background and the climate and culture of our land. They showed the Catholic world in Europe what the faith could mean to an American. They showed their fellow Americans that they were a part of America, a part possessed of fire and wisdom that America could not do without.

Catholics clung to each other because a man in a ghetto has no other choice. They clung together longer than was needed because, like frightened children in war, they could not believe that the bombs and screaming rockets had ceased. The echoes were still in their ears, the bitterness still in their mouths, the memories of Al Smith and Boston's Brahmins locked in their hearts. They were too proud of their victories, too defensive in their defeats, but it was not hard to understand their feelings if you saw their scars. Their pastors were sergeants who led them into battle and gave them courage and hope. They told them to build schools and they built them with the fury of a father building a shelter for his children. They told them to heed the bishop and the Pope, and they followed their words with the determination of a man in all-out war.[2] That war, however, is over, and another has begun, the war of civilized man to survive and live in peace. In such a world religious differences sound like the persistent whinings of a spoiled child. And still we build our schools and beg for funds to perpetuate an America which we have fought to bury in the past.

We build our schools like soldiers returning from the war who learned only to fight. We build them to honor the wisdom of another age. We build them to please our parents, to thank our pastors for their service and their love, to make our bishops happy, to postpone the religious problems that presently we face. We beg for more vocations to fill our schools with teachers, when we should begin to close them and send our priests and sisters to more important fields. We ignore our children in the public schools and offer them irrelevant programs of catechism that only leave them bored.[3] We ignore the state universities and the religious indifference that challenges our students there. We build schools to protect the Catholic children from the world in which they live, to smother them with religious information they do not really need. We build, we build, we build, even though the coming generation will find our schools obsolete.

No longer can we protect our children from their society, no longer will Catholics remain separate in the world in which they live. They need religion, they even want it, if their conversation is any indication of their appetite. They wonder about morality, ponder values, question the power of God, sense the sacred in the joy and the emptiness of life. They need religion, but they do not need our schools.

I have taught in parochial schools for more than ten years. I have taught children in grade school and young adults in the Catholic university. I have been a staunch defender of Catholic education and pressured many a student away from the state university, where he would be exposed to the "temptations of the world." I continued to sell Catholic education long after I personally questioned the defensiveness of its message and the quality of its religious formation. I argued that a sound education should include theology, even though I knew that Catholic schools only offer advanced catechism and largely irrelevant moralizing. I fought those who questioned Catholic schools. I spoke of the dangerous positivism that infected our universities, the pagan perspectives that soiled our lusting world. I saw Catholic schools as the hope of our civilization, the last fortress in a raging world of sin. Then, suddenly, I stopped defending and started to think.

What difference was there between the students I taught in the parochial high school every day and those from the public schools who attended my evening discussion once a week? The public-school students were as sincere and searching as any I ever taught. They were perhaps more tolerant than those in parochial schools, less indifferent about their faith, more mature in their awareness of the modern world. Their morals seemed as solid as the substance of their home. They brought their Protestant and Jewish friends to hear our discussions and encouraged them to state their views. They attended Mass, struggled to respect their parents, planned to attend college and to have loving families of their own.

They made me wonder if information is as important a part of religious training as I had been led to believe. What part does theology have in the building of a faith? Does any child need more than a smattering of theology unless he reveals an aptitude or interest in such a discipline? Is it not more important that a young person have a chance to practice religion, such as working with the poor, than to master definitions and to know the names of Abraham's wives? Religious instruction is one thing and religion quite another.

These children in the public schools were not concerned with the involved dogmas that occupied my class time in the parochial school. They did not care about the distinction between actual and sanctifying grace, the refined discussions about sacraments and angels, the gifts of the Holy Spirit, or the latest findings on the Galileo case. They were bored with the textbook I provided to cover the whole of our system in four years of Thursday evenings from seven till eight. They wanted religion; not facts about it, not involved studies about it, but something to give them courage and to provide meaning for their life. If I spoke of the "sacrament of initiation" they were fidgety, if I talked of "salvation history" they were bored. They didn't want to know that they were "prophet, priest and king"; they wanted to know that they were alive and capable of love. I could not tell them of the meaning of the Exodus, or rehash the story of Moses, or else they'd "turn me off." I had to begin with Kennedy to discover Moses, and to speak of novels and movies if Abraham was to live.

And yet, each morning for four long hours, I taught religion in the parochial school. For most of the students this was only tolerable because my classes were more exciting than the dull catechism they had had in the past. They were the victims of a Catholic grade school where untrained sisters taught a theology they themselves had never understood. I do not blame the sisters; I am in envy of their patient endurance. But most of them knew no theology, and a questioning hand could mean a stuttering effort to defend the Church. No wonder the students could tolerate my class. Some even liked it, just as some are fond of history or math. The majority, however, were bored and resentful of the discussions, which had little bearing on their lives. They had heard of the Trinity until it exuded from their ears. They had discussed the death of Christ until they knew the mark of every nail. They knew the pains of hell, the rights of marriage, the purpose of confirmation, the seven deadly sins, the beauty of Mary, and the heritage of Adam and Eve.

They were bored, and so was I. I was preparing little information boxes who could pass tests and challenge the evangelists who knocked on their doors. Of what value was this?[4] Did it make them more concerned with the horror of war, the suffering of the poor, the injustice to the Negro, the frantic pace of modern life which gave no time for self-knowledge and peace? Would it make them better spouses or citizens, would it make them more human, more attuned to the mystery of life? Or did it only make them smug and righteous, narrowminded and afraid? I was giving them information when they wanted life. I was providing them with answers when they were not even open to the questions that honest men asked.

So I changed my approach and devised my own course. I abandoned the textbook and taught in seminar fashion. We read selections from *Time* and *Look*, pondered the meaning of *Catcher in the Rye* and *1984*. We examined Françoise Sagan, Hemingway, and William James.[5] We attended and discussed movies, and when I recommended *The Silence* by Bergman, I almost lost my job. I abandoned exams and quizzes, and marked them on a single essay on "The Search for Self in Modern Society." I marked liberally, paid little attention to rhetoric and spelling, encouraged freedom of expression, perhaps even rebellion. I discovered, however, that I was only trying to repair the damage done by the narrow Catholic ghetto and to create the experience that other students found in their public schools. Half of my time was spent in fighting intolerance or arrogance, or the bigotry of frightened parents. I was teaching students who had been trained by Catholic teachers, who had read largely Catholic books, and were immersed in Catholic experience. And yet they would go on to live in a world where men are only men.

Some of them would marry non-Catholics, some would lose their faith, some would find an answer in humanism, some would investigate another religion, some would settle into the routine observance of a dull Catholicism. Some would love their faith, some would grow to despise it. Girls would get pregnant and "have to get married." Boys would go in service and abandon religious practice. Some would practice birth control, others would shun it. Some would get divorced, others would know the beauty of a Christian home. But what did I contribute by my high-school classes? Was I solving any problems, or only postponing them? Was I forming their faith or had it been well determined by the family in which they lived?

Even the recent surveys cannot justify the money we spend for Catholic schools. And in effect, surveys are of little worth, because there is no possible way to measure what is mature faith and what is merely indoctrination. Surveys can tell us who goes to Mass, but they cannot tell us what happens to man in the center of his soul. They cannot reduce honesty to a graph nor chart the fire of charity nor distinguish between honest action and empty words. But even though surveys cannot justify our system of parochial schools, bishops and pastors continue to build their monuments.

How is a child better formed in a parochial school than in an intelligent program of part-time religious education after school? [6] We really don't know, since we have never had an intelligent part-time program. We spend millions of dollars on our Catholic schools and pennies on the greater number of Catholics who attend our public schools. Meanwhile, a few battered heroes try to convince our stubborn bishops that the Church faces a crisis in religious education.[7] These few recognize how little we have done for our students in public schools and how vastly their number is growing. Bishops continue to appoint diocesan directors of religious education who are "safe" and without professional training in the field, or who have accumulated sudden and unquestioned wisdom in a summer-seminar. Education is obviously among the most explosive problems we face, and I am convinced that if we developed a sound program for teaching religion to Catholic students in public schools, we could phase out the bulk of our own schools in twenty years.

You cannot possibly know the agony of this situation unless you have worked for the Catholic Church. Our leaders will not face the problem! They extoll our Catholic schools without having taught in one recently—if ever—and without any measuring stick of their effectiveness. They complain that public-school students will not attend our part-time classes, without realizing how niggardly have been our efforts to make such classes interesting and relevant. They only imagine that they face the problem when they gather a few sisters and overworked priests to develop a program. They join them with a few gifted professors and some interested publishers and ask them to improve the textbooks and outlines. This assembled body works for three or four days, glows with mutual admiration, and continues to provide us with more printed irrelevance. And why not? They have been asked to do a full-time job on a part-time basis. They have been asked to resolve a key and perhaps desperate situation without adequate authority or charter. When will we face the problem and gather the very best of our talent into authorized full-time teams to explore the psychology, the sociology, the theology, and the philosophy of religious education? When will we learn something of the modern techniques of communications? When will we be bold enough to experiment, to recognize decay, to realize that the forms which served our parents and grandparents have been outgrown?

Our bishops would not stumble so if the question were one of diocesan finance, if parochial income dropped 25 percent. But with education our frightened bishops hesitate. They continue to build more schools, when they should bury them because this is a new and exciting era in the Church. Pope John lived with us long enough to tell us that we can join the rest of the world in a search for vision and value. Even the fears of Pope Paul, the foot-dragging of Vatican II, and the largely irrelevant concerns of our American bishops in their recent conference cannot dull the memory of John. He changed our outlook, opened our hearts, quieted our fears, and in essence told us that we could close our "segregated" schools.

Some of our schools will always survive, but they will have

to be monuments to the best in private education and not the barricades that preserve fear, intolerance, prejudice, and weak inbreeding. We no longer want to hear the letters from our bishops each summer reminding us of the necessity of parochial schools. Nor will we ever jam our classrooms with every last child to save his soul from a pagan and faithless world. We must chisel out our faith in common with the rest of mankind, and our Church must offer us relevant programs of religious education independently of school. In fact, if we rejoined the world of our countrymen and showed them that we have the best interest of our nation at heart, there well might come courses of religion offered as electives in our public schools.

No longer must every religious order feel compelled to erect its special schools or colleges to shelter three or four hundred girls. To build such a school today is to erect a monument to a holy founder or to satisfy the ego needs of an order or a weary, nostalgic superior. We would do well gradually to sell many of our schools—not just one or two of them—to the public, and with the compensation we could give our talent and attention to the religious problems of our age. We could permit our gifted priests and sisters to teach in secular universities and to prove the fire of their commitment by the breadth of their open mindedness. We could even close most of our seminary colleges and encourage our fledgling priests to discover how the rest of the world thinks and lives. We could open our remaining universities to the scholars of other creeds and values in order to discover what are truly the questions of our times. Why are there only one or two Protestant theologians at Catholic universities? [8] Why are there so few theological schools at our state universities? Mainly because theology has been a frightened and defensive discipline, afraid to meet in open discussion the questions which a man must face in the barbershop or cocktail lounge. What are we afraid of? Truth? Or are we afraid that we will lose the man who wonders and doubts? If so, we have lost him already, because we do not have the confidence to admit that God can draw man in His own way. I can honestly say that I did not really believe in a mature manner until I read Barth and Tillich, Calvin and Luther, Kierkegaard, Buber, and Camus. Faith can grow in Freud and Nietzsche, Dewey and James, Sartre and Heidegger. It only ceases to grow in fear and narrowness and never in the energy of an honest search. Such a search is the very mark of our age, and we recognize it once we emerge from the ghetto of WASP and Catholic and discover that each man's blood is only red.

In a modern age, most of our schools will pass away, but they will not leave without a fight. The very money invested in them is the strongest motive involved in retaining them. This is a sad commentary on a great and historic Church which prefers to grow irrelevant rather than abandon the schools which only serve to tell weak men that their work has not been in vain. They need the symbols that indicate success, regardless of how unnecessary such symbols have become.

Actually, our grade schools should be the first to go, since the religious formation of the young is so obviously the product of home environment! The religious needs of children can well be handled in part-time religious programs. This would give us an immediate chance to reduce the strain on religious vocations, and to take the time to develop new methods of Christian service. We could, perhaps, attempt to transform some of our high schools into true models of the best in education and honesty, but preserve only those that can demonstrate their value. They should be servants of the community and the nation, and should admit a representative number of students and teachers of other faiths.[9] Short of this, ecumenism is just so much talk. With the demise of our grade schools we would have to come up with sound programs of part-time religious education, and not flounder as we have in the past. We should have the same courage to thin out our colleges and universities as we had in building them, and to erect a new college should never again be the prerogative of some local octogenarian or megalomaniac. No bishop or religious superior, acting with misguided zeal, should be able to impose upon an unaware people a financial drive to build an educational irrelevance. We have far too many already. Dioceses and religious institutions should have the courage and wisdom to assess their educational institutions of all varieties and ask the simple question: "Why?"

We must abandon our schools with the same historic insight that pushed us to erect them. Such dynamic change has ever marked the history of the Church. We have been stubborn and slow, as a giant body must ever be, but we have not been afraid to change. Once the monks did not hesitate to teach the people to farm, and then to build. They taught boys to read and to conjugate when there was no other way. They were willing to be beggars or soldiers and knights if the service of man seemed to warrant it. The sisters were willing to nurse soldiers or lepers, to gather orphans, to care for unwed mothers, to bathe the children of the poor. There were orders of preachers to stem religious ignorance and superstition, or to provide teachers for the growing universities of Paris, Salamanca, and Louvain. There were friars who taught the people to build roads, or who, in poverty, spoke without any words. They wrote books and they also burned them, they chided, scolded, and extolled. There were the special troops of the Pope and commandos of each council, ready to serve man as time and circumstances said he must be served.

Now the change must occur once again, and man must be served with new ways, and not with the services that he in his society has outgrown. There are special areas where no one has yet recognized the needs and pains of man. Here must Christianity come alive with the principles of creative love that helped to heal another generation. Perhaps we are expected to pour our energies into the world of poverty and the plight of the Negro. What would be the result if the Church of Bernard and Borromeo, Elizabeth of Hungary and Vincent de Paul began to channel its mighty forces into the education of the poor? What if our sisters were to walk among them in great numbers, to cook and clean for them, to fight for them, to teach and console without the obvious prospects of conversion? Would they fear the threat to a virginity which means nothing locked in a convent? And could not the Church teach us to live in a world of speed and machines, to find peace amid tension, culture amid leisure, simplicity and personal love in the midst of rising incomes?

Must we have a particular and special work that we do not share with others? Or has man, perhaps, moved so far in twenty centuries that we can only join with those who do the work that once was exclusively ours? Once we ran the hospitals, the orphanages, the homes for lepers, and the schools for children. Now man has matured to recognize his responsibility as man. Can we not be grateful that it is difficult to recognize a Christian in our society since so many men and women do Christian work? Is there no work for a parish without fences, for a Church without schools. Once we were the Church of the poor and the hungry. How came we to be the Church of the middle class? Can we not search for the modern men who are blind and deaf and lame in modern ways? Once man cried to us for schools and Catholic Youth Organizations and even boxing gloves. Now he cries for mental health and happy marriages and friendship in a world of computers and space.

Is it not time to abandon some of our inherited structures and to search and explore? Long enough have we ignored the religious problems of state universities, to teach innocent communicants how to fold their hands and to memorize meaningless prayers.[10] Long enough have we equated religion with education and lost our vision for the vast works that have not been done. I worked, for example, in a large parish in New York City teeming with the aged. The parish offered a lecture series, a parish mission, but nothing for the bored old folks who went to Mass, confession, and the park because they had nowhere else to go. Maybe we should run lunch counters or bars. Maybe we should run laundromats or coffeehouses and card rooms. Maybe we should work in television and on the stage.

I know a hundred places we should be, and you can tell me a hundred more. But we will never get there if we are afraid to abandon our inherited structures. We do not live in a world in which we can protect Catholics, not even one in which we can serve Catholics alone. We know that every man is our charge and we must serve him where he needs us. We must reexamine our goals, no matter the cost. We are not here to convert the world, but to serve it. We are not even here to save souls, but to love all men. God will convert and save in His good time.

It is a time to question and to surge ahead. It is time to search out the helpless and the weak and to go to them, no matter their poverty or affluence, no matter their faith or lack of it. It is a time to ignore statistics, which have hypnotized and impressed us. It is time to forget about finances, to canonize no form, to seek no credit, to work without ceasing. It is time to do almost anything except, please God, to build more Catholic schools.

12. LIFE IN THE CONVENT

Several years ago a nun approached me with a serious problem of conscience. She had been struggling with a sexual temptation that left her tormented and confused. Although she had lived as a nun for twenty years, suddenly she could not work or sleep for fear that she had been unfaithful to her vows. It took courage and cunning for her to contact me, since such private consultations were not encouraged in her order. She was expected to receive permission for each and every visit with a priest and to travel with a sister companion between convent and rectory. It was apparently not safe for her to come alone. I had first learned of her problem when I dropped by her classroom one day after school to borrow a dictionary. She asked if it would be possible to see me privately sometime and then she began to cry.

I learned that she had struggled with her secret fear for almost three years, until she felt that she was living perpetually in "mortal sin." I asked her why she had not talked the matter over with a priest in confession. She informed me that the assigned confessor was always in a hurry and was not the kind of man with whom one discussed such a problem. Besides, as I later learned, it was not the kind of problem that one would want to discuss in the darkness of the confessional, but the kind that would have to be worked out gradually in a counseling situation. When I told her that I would be happy to see her at any convenient time, she laughed bitterly amid her tears. It was then she told me the special and difficult arrangements that would be necessary. She would have to approach her superior like a little girl and reveal in some detail the reason for her request. The mother superior looked upon such "special permissions" as a sad reflection on the happy community life for which she was responsible. If problems existed, they were to be kept within the convent walls and not to be televised to the world. The superior, a woman of sixty, without an ounce of psychology or human relations in her background, was the "mother confessor" of this group of sixteen nuns. The sisters were "called in" for private conferences, they were at times reprimanded for a lack of family spirit, for giddiness or individualism, for failure in the spirit of prayer or personal asceticism. Since they could bare their souls to such an interested "mother," there was really no need of outside help.

Finally, we did arrange a series of visits in my office while the sister companion busied herself in the waiting room with correcting papers and repairing her winter shawl. It was not long before I decided that the problem was out of my province. When I suggested that sister should see a psychiatrist, she wept without control. Such a recommendation was out of the question, not because she could not admit this need to herself, but because the mother superior, a sturdy and disciplined immigrant, would not be able to understand. Another nun in the convent had asked for such help, and she had never been permitted to forget it. So I ended up doing the best I could with the advice of a psychiatrist friend. In the course of our conversations it became clear that sister knew little or nothing about her own sexual makeup and it was hard to discuss "sexual sins" without some further education. I gave her a couple of books to read despite her protests, and she hid them like a child with dirty pictures. I asked a physician to prescribe tranquilizers without knowing the sister to whom they were given.

It was a mad arrangement in an incredible structure, which, unfortunately, was not an unusual exception.

Later that year the sister was moved to another parish and found it increasingly difficult to continue the visits. The new "mother superior" was a boisterous back-slapper who thought that the solution to every emotional problem was fresh air and a hearty laugh. When I did manage to see sister, I felt like I was preparing for some furtive affair, so carefully did our plans have to be laid. For a time I could not write to her since her letters were censored. When she wrote to me, she did it secretly and mailed the letters with surreptitious caution. Gradually she did show some improvement, but still needed a great deal of help when our paths became permanently divided.

I wish that such a case were atypical. It well may be dramatic and, today, of less frequent occurrence, but it is not exceptional or exaggerated. Sisters do occasionally have serious problems which have been obscured or ignored lest such bad public relations should impair the flow of vocations. I remember the sister who was having a problem with homosexuality calling me from a pay station in a drugstore, and I ended up hearing her confession in the library stacks of a state university so that she would not have to receive permission to go to confession. I have heard sisters' confessions while walking across the school yard, in an empty classroom, at an altar boys' picnic. Canon law tells me that I cannot hear such confessions validly outside of the confessional, but common sense tells me that no man or woman is bound to the impossible. Canon law also provides numerous freedoms for a sister who requires confession, but experience has made me know that such freedoms are often not worth the paper on which they appear.[1] I do not mean to imply that sisters are frequently troubled by serious moral problems. I merely state that they sometimes are, and the structure of convent life then puts them through the terrors of the damned.

Once upon a time the rules of convent life were, perhaps, not unreasonable. Once the great majority of nuns in our country were the peasant children of immigrants and pioneers. They had learned in their large and disciplined families to sacrifice feelings, to live without privacy, to prize unquestioning obedience as the supreme sign of humility and faith. They had been taught to work hard, to ignore personal needs, to bury emotions in silence and a nervous smile. The white-haired pastor of the parish was Moses on a mountain with his arms raised high, filled with the spirit of private and public infallibility. Their natural father was also a man of self-denial and few complaints. To such women, religious life was not really a unique challenge, but merely a continuation of the existence they had known in the structured family of their neat and theocratic world.

Many of these women became nuns because they were enlisted by the solemn and strong priest who controlled their lives. They had really never thought of marriage, they knew little if anything of sex, and many knew from life at home that matrimony meant merely discipline and self-denial. They had seen their fathers work a dozen hours a day in factory or field. They had known the weary mothers who scrubbed, baked, and rubbed their rosaries until they drifted off to bed. There had been no talk of personal and ecstatic love, no word about the drive and violent hunger of the flesh, no deep discussions about the need for fulfillment in life. These were the hardy daughters whose mothers fed the chickens the morning after they bore a baby. They were the daughters of the potato farmers and dock workers, the progeny of wagon trains and crowded ships that landed in New York.

I knew these women well, and know the few that linger still. They taught me and encouraged me in my vocation. They spoke of the Cross with shining eyes and carried it with the asceticism learned as children. They could bury feelings without obvious frustration. They could pass from a position of authority to a drone's job in the ranks without upset. They could live a life without privacy, perform a task for which they were neither suited nor educated. They could teach subjects they had never formally learned, teach when they wanted to nurse, cook when they longed to work among the poor. They could retire at an hour when the rest of the world was beginning to seek out entertainment and culture. They could rise when the rest of the world was resting for another day. They could teach children with only a vague idea of the life the children lived. Forbidden to visit private homes, they could miss their mother's funeral or a golden jubilee. They were content not to attend a wedding nor be seen in public after dark simply because they were not allowed to.

All of this they seemed willingly to do in the name of the Church and the holy founder who had devised their rule. Their "holy rule," too, was the product of culture and folkways long since dead. They somehow lacked the freedom to change the inspired words of this rule which well may have been modern in the days of surreys and kerosene lamps. They attempted to run schools without questioning a proud pastor's ignorant interference. They taught school all year and picked up a degree over ten or twenty summers. They went to Mass every day whether they wanted to or not. They made eight-day retreats without speaking a word. They guarded the pride of their order no matter the personal cost. They competed for vocations and nursed the special students who seemed to be destined for the convent life. They prayed far more than they studied, even though they had been called to an active life within scholastic halls. They accepted sixty children in a classroom in order to please the pastor or his parish, and sometimes believed the myth that a nun can handle such numbers because of her special touch. They were the marvelous women who taught our fathers, and their fathers, and even some of us.

But gradually, even suddenly, they were invaded by the young sisters who had not known the world of the washboard and sacrifice. Yet the rules were unwilling or unable to change.[2] The new breed were the daughters of doctors and insurance men, draftsmen, dentists, and factory foremen. They had known freedom and trust, dances and spending money. They had read modern authors, attended "B" movies, and even traveled to Europe. Their presence precipitated a clash and I witnessed it a thousand times.

I shall never forget the sister assigned in one parish to teach math. She had been a good student but had not a particle of interest in cosines and logarithms. In the four years I knew her she grew alternately fat and thin, pale, despondent, and wretched. She came to me one day to tell me that she wanted to leave the convent. I asked if she had taken the matter up with her superiors. She informed me that her request had not been taken seriously since the order was short of teachers and had trained no one else to teach math. She told me, haltingly, as one quite unaccustomed to honest and personal communication, that once she had wanted to be a nun who labored among the sick and poor. She had made her request known on several occasions, but had repeatedly been told that God wanted her for another work. Before she entered the convent officially, she had been assured that she would be able to do the work that had filled her dreams. After her training, however, it had been suggested that she deposit her personal judgment in a superior's hands. So she continued to say her prayers and teach her math until she almost lost her balance.

In many ways she was afraid to leave the convent. The superior could make her departure so complicated and guilt-ridden that it would hardly be worth the personal strain. It was easier, in some ways, to drift along and call her life a "cross," when her whole being cried out for something else.[3] The really frightening thing was that there was actually no honest avenue of recourse. She could go to the pastor of the parish, but he was most likely baptized in the same system of "devotion to duty" and "God's will" that stifled communication with her own superior. Besides, he needed a math teacher and sisters come a whole lot cheaper than lay teachers. Her own superior would not offer much sympathy, since dissatisfaction within the community would threaten the superior's own prominence and authority within the order. Each superior must run a "happy family" or headquarters would likely take the matter amiss. It may happen, too, that the superior has some doubts about her own vocation, and the distress of a young sister can threaten her personal security. This was true in the case under discussion, and every visit to the superior produced more confusion and guilt, as the young sister was told of her selfishness and her stubborn rejection of "God's many graces." She was further told not to make her dissatisfaction known to the other sisters, since this, too, could upset the equanimity of a happy home.

Perhaps you, a product of a world of personal responsibility and decision, would ask: "Why doesn't she just walk out?" You, however, do not understand. "God's will" and "sacrifice" are words of deep meaning within the system and can frighten even the most independent and courageous. Besides, where would this sister go and what would she do? Her family would, most likely, mourn her departure. They had seen her as the flowering of their own faith and personal sacrifice. She was the daughter that they had given to God, their "bargaining point" at Heaven's gate. In addition, she had been sheltered from the world for a dozen years, and I do mean sheltered.[4] She had no friendships, she was not trained to make personal decisions, she had not a penny of income nor the money even to buy clothes. She would likely leave the convent like a convict, wearing the clothes she brought in or a simple outfit that some recent recruit had abandoned in the dressing room. She did not know how to go about getting a job or renting an apartment, nor would the order feel the least responsibility to make her leave-taking pleasant, or even untraumatic. She would be asked not to say good-bye to her fellow sisters, she would be hurried out of sight like an embarrassing relative, and the children she taught would be told that she was moved to another assignment. All the while she would not be sure that she had done the right thing, since her mind was confused and unsettled. She still was not sure that she did not have a "vocation," so carefully had the mystique of a "religious vocation" been buried in pious nonsense. She was only sure that she had been unhappy and lost. One understanding hand stretched out to help her might well be enough to lead her to peace, but she could well linger in years of misery before she found it. She was permitted to talk to no one who might understand, no one who was not conditioned by the system or personal frustration and fear. All she would hear would be: "Hang on and God will provide!" And if some priest or doctor were to make the exit smooth and easy, he would likely never receive a referral from this order again. I know, because I gave her the money to leave, and found her a respectable job.

I am not giving archaic examples. I had a very similar case a year ago in one of the most "modern" and "renewed" orders. I had taught theology to this young lady, and she had come to me a year later hoping that I would understand. When she finally had summoned up the courage to demand her release from "temporary" vows, a process which can be simple or vastly complicated, she was "forced" to take a teaching position in a distant state for five months. While she was preparing to leave for her new assignment, she was locked in a room so that she would not make contact with any of her sister friends. She wrote me from her new assignment to tell me of her utter misery. She did not want to be a nun and yet she was forced to live the life for several months while her "case" was being pushed through channels. The "channels" could have been opened in ten minutes, but a teacher was needed and she was unwillingly sent. Her letter ended with the words: "I don't know how long I can hang on. I just don't know!"

There are many sisters who would like to leave the convent. They came to convent life in obedience to some mysterious and "divine" command, or in fear of marriage or spinsterhood. They came to win a parent's love, to feel important, to avoid personal decisions, to fulfill a youthful vow, to prevent a sensitive conscience from tearing them apart. They came in youthful daydreams or unable to resist the pressures of a pastor, a parent, the nun who knew them for several years. Or perhaps they came searching for peace, which seemed to elude them everywhere. They came to escape confusion or decision, or to create a goal. They discovered after a year or ten that they should not remain, and they tried to summon up the courage to be honest to themselves. Many, perhaps most, could not leave, so they settled into the busy routine that alternately soothes and tortures them. After a time they do not question or think, they just drift along knowing that life can no longer offer them anything else.

There are thousands, too, who came and remained because they had found the life for which they were apparently destined. They accepted its difficulties even as they looked forward to renewal. They found in it a life of fulfillment and meaning. They grew in love and peace, they moved each person they met with admiration and a strange awareness of the presence of God. My close friend Sister "Jean" is such a nun, sensitive, intelligent, open, and totally feminine. She can talk as easily about the joys as about the difficulties and empty formalism of convent life. She is not afraid to love individuals and to tell them of her love. She was not afraid to tell me. She is not defensive about her habit, her rule, or her total way of life. She can laugh at the uniform which marks a nun as one who is obviously out of contact with the world. She can ridicule the changes in dress, adopted after many meetings and prayers, which hardly alter the medieval image. She can dream of the convents of the future, in which the sisters will be able to make friends easily and will be trusted to live as mature and independent women. She admits the diminishing number of vocations without "contrived" explanations, and sees in it a sign of progress. She approves the programs which teach a young sister about personal motivation, hidden sources of guilt, and the latent fears of sex and marriage.

She can speak of a convent life in which each nun does not have to walk alike and hide her hands or bury her personality in the rules provided by a well-meaning foundress.[5] She speaks of the need for freedom and privacy, if the sister is truly to be an active woman in the world. She looks forward to the day when the sister will not be locked from the world's sight once darkness falls, and will not be forced to rise in group conformity for Mass and morning prayers. Community has to mean more than compulsory programs of prayer and girlish recreation. The nun of the future should be able to know the joy of personal decision and to establish her own rule of life within the framework of the religious family.

Sister "Jean," like many other sisters, feels the need for personal friendships. She told me of a convent in which she was assigned where there was no sister who shared her age or interests. She was obliged to share her free time with the "community," although the "community" was only four other nuns. The superior of the convent was well past sixty-five, kind, gentle, and completely out of touch with the world. Her idea of real fun was to sew or to surprise "Father" on his feast day. Two of the other sisters were extreme introverts incapable of speaking personally at all. They lived as if they had no feelings. The other sister, who did most of the cooking and housework, was in her dotage, and spent her free time humming Christmas carols or saying her rosary while watching TV. This was "Jean's" home for four years, and her contacts with lay people were restricted to chats with mothers after Mass or school. She was not permitted to attend a movie theater (unless *Bambi* was being rerun) or a private home, since the mother superior did not consider this "prudent" behavior for a dedicated nun. (Mother Superior was not required to explain what "prudent" actually meant.) On one occasion "Jean" was visited by a young bachelor who taught in the public high school, and the superior told her to discourage any further calls.

Life in the convent needs renewal more desperately than any form of Catholic life.[6] Nowhere in the Church have the personnel invested more of themselves. Nowhere in the Church are they quite as lacking in avenues of recourse. For years, we priests were able to treat nuns as disembodied spirits who somehow did not need the vacations, the outlets, the relaxation demanded by the clergy. We could ask of them working and living conditions that we would never expect of ourselves. When I suffered most from an irate and impossible pastor or an overwhelming work load, I could always get away. I could chase the golf ball, have a few beers, or relax for three weeks in Miami. The sisters, however, must return to the convent and join in the common prayer or common meals or common recreation. It has often not been important how they feel, or how they like their job, or to what extent the "community" can tear them apart. They have been the "dear nuns," the "good sisters," the gentle little anachronisms without feeling. The standard procedure in many parishes has been to ignore their complaints until they disappear, or at best to offer some token and fleeting redress.

Once upon a time the sisters were able to say that they were the "brides of Christ" in a kind of spirituality fashioned before Freud. They could fix upon the contrived image of some misty, historical Christ who was a product of their dreams and not the healthy vision of a living and relevant Christian. They could linger before the tabernacle as a patient spouse waiting for her "man" to come home or to communicate with a Christ born in a stable of sugar and spice. They could make of Christ whatever kind of bridegroom they wanted Him to be and hide their frustrations in their "personal love" for Him. At times they could find a "father" in the pastor, a "mother" in the religious superior, in a superb and involved effort to avoid maturity and growth. Once such innocence and childlike deference was acceptable, even touching, in the simplicity that it produced. Of late it has grown pathetic and out of date.

Christ took no spouse except the Church,[7] nor did He need a bride to keep Him "company" in the morning or at night. He needed free and healthy laborers in His vineyard, women whose life, and even whose garb and attitude, is modern and meaningful. No girl can account for her every thought, her every minute, her every dime, and become a woman. She must be free enough to make mistakes, modern enough to be a real woman, and human enough to form male and female friends outside the convent walls. She must have money to spend,[8] time to travel, a chance to be alone, and to be, at times, anonymous in a crowd. She must not hide behind her robes, must not be led to believe that she walks on the streets as a symbol of dedication when she is only a sign of an outmoded tradition. She must not bury her personality in the tired rules of some long-dead foundress. She must be free to enter the convent and must be given both encouragement and tangible support when she chooses to leave. She must know that she is first a child of God and only then a daughter of her parents, her pastor, her religious community.

It would do her good to have dinner with a man, to speak personally to him. It would do the world good to know that she can accept human love and still want to be a nun. Presently, most nuns would be forbidden to ride in the front seat of a car with a priest or embarrassed to have a snack with him in a quiet café. A vocation cannot be a burial from the world as once it was. It must spring from a mature love, a dedication, and not from a high wall of protections and fears. There are women in the world who know a virgin's dedication without knowing a nun's inhibited existence. There are nurses and teachers, social workers and cooks in rest homes who live without marriage in peace and honest fulfillment.

We do not have to "crowd" our young women for vocations or force the religious life on the frightened and the passively docile. There may not be so many nuns in a world which permits them to live as free women, but there will be more than enough to do the work. Their very life will be attractive enough to continue to draw the courageous and deep woman who seeks more than marriage can give in terms of service and human concern. Then the world will not wonder about them and check them off as the frustrated virgins who march without "oil" or "lamps." They will not be the oddities that wander through our streets with their umbrellas and black bags. They will not be the conversation stoppers that hear only half of the world's ways. They will be the magnificent women that some have managed to be despite unbelievable obstacles, the mature and relevant sisters who search out the lonely and the poor, who speak of God without uttering a pious phrase or handing out a single "holy card," who know even more about this world than they do about the next. Then they can begin to speak of "community," and even I will know what they mean.

13. THE MAN WHO IS A NON-CATHOLIC

From childhood through my priesthood, I have learned that every non-Catholic is a potential Catholic. He has no other meaning. The hope of his conversion is the reason for the smile I offer him, the kind word I whisper when I pass. If he lives in my neighborhood, I must convert him by my example; if he lives in China, I must convert him by my prayers. The non-Catholic is the target of a never-ending conspiracy to drag him unawares to Rome. If he resists my efforts, time will undoubtedly tell him of the heresy that blinds and fetters him, and I will ignore him and search out his more docile children.

A non-Catholic is not a Jew who holds dear the faith and history of his people. He is simply not a Catholic, and I must lead him patiently to truth. The non-Catholic is not a committed Protestant who loves his neighbor and worships his God. He is not a Catholic, and is deprived of the strength and comfort of the Church. A non-Catholic is not an honest searcher who lives without the structure of organized faith. He is a pagan, a cripple, who will never learn to love until he finds the path to Rome. All of this I learned in my parochial school, in the seminary which trained me to be a priest. I learned it from my fellow priests in serious conversation and seminars, in the talk over beer, in the treatment of non-Catholics by the rulings of my Church.

I learned my lesson well and practiced it carefully in my labors as a priest. I remember the sad-faced lady who used to wait for me each Sunday after the final Mass. She was well-dressed, lived in a beautiful home, had two bright and healthy children, was married to an interesting and thoughtful husband. Yet she was a tragic figure, and I helped to make her so. It was not her health or her job that upset her. It was the husband who did not share her faith. He was a non-Catholic who stubbornly resisted the power of her prayers and the charm of my approach. She waited after Mass because she knew her husband would soon be there to pick her up. She would delay me that he might have another chance to know the hypnotic influence of the Catholic priest. Maybe this time he would see the folly of his ways, and know the mystery and joy he missed. So we stood there, the sad-faced lady and I, waiting for her husband to return from the golf course, that we might invite him by our presence to the sacred rites of Rome.

He always drove up to the back door of the Church with a style all his own. He bounced from the car with a special exuberance, shook my hand with a big grin, and said, "Think my old lady will ever amount to anything, Father?" We all laughed, but the lady and I wondered if God would ever hear our prayers, or if only the threat of death would move this non-Catholic to join the one, true Church.

He was a good husband, an involved and loving father, but a heartache to his wife. My Church had made him her heartache, and so had I, by pushing her to struggle for his conversion. And when he resisted, in his kind and manly way, she questioned her prayers, her daily example, the sincerity of the penances she offered in his behalf. And in her eyes each Sunday after Mass I saw her pleading and her hurt. She was counting on me because her husband liked my personality and my interest in their children. I was her new hope, her last champion, the strong knight who could challenge her husband in the battlefield of religion and lead him to the Church. She invited me to dinner. She telephoned me, to recount each religious suggestion that slipped from his unsuspecting lips. She prayed ceaselessly and told the children that they must storm heaven with the fervor of their requests. She sent money to missionaries, who promised to help her with their labors and prayers in another land. She had Masses said for a "special intention," exulted when he joined her on Christmas and Easter in the pew, rejoiced when he glanced at the Catholic literature she had strewn carefully through the house.

But somehow he resisted, read his Bible almost every day, and continued to love his family without the guidance of my Church. Now I wonder how he could smile when we badgered him with the pressure of our frantic attack. We had forced him to sign promises that he would raise his children in the Catholic faith. We had embarrassed his parents when we refused to marry him at the altar of our Church. He had submitted to the instructions provided to explain our "position" and to hasten his "conversion." He had endured the requests of his little children when they asked him to join them in their first communion and to pray with them at Mass. He had tried to answer their questions of why he was not a Catholic, or how he would get to heaven without the priest. Yet he smiled, this man that we had made a stranger in his house.

His wife had signed no promises to respect his honor and dignity in the home he built. She was not required to tell the children that men could serve God in many different ways. She was not obliged to explain that his loyalty was the product of faith and his love its inner core. She had only promised to convert him, to lead him from the folly of his simple and incomplete religion, and to see that he did not win the children to the poverty of his own, misguided state.

Once, history tells us, Omar and his Muhammadan hordes forced conversions at the tip of the sword. They threatened Christians and dragged frightened Catholics to pray and worship in the mosque. And when we read such bloody and bar-

baric accounts we shudder, somehow forgetting the swords we wield in Spain and the daggers we thrust in the heart of the non-Catholic husband with the sad-faced wife. Our daggers are everywhere, and we use them with artistic skill. We poise them before each non-Catholic who hopes to take a Catholic spouse, before Protestant parents who watch their children marry in our Church. We poise them before the Jews, even as we smile at them and ignore their traditions, which are as sacred and deep-rooted as our own. We poise them before the millions who find Churches a sham and organized religion a study of hypocrisy. We poise them before the world, at the United Nations, at welfare conferences, at the ecumenical gatherings where we feign brotherhood and are not prepared to budge an inch. Our daggers, perhaps, are more secret than Omar's sword, but not less painful. The non-Catholic feels their sharp steel in every contact with the Catholic Church.

We might fool the Protestant observers who attended Vatican II, or lull to sleep the Jews who receive a blessed medallion in an audience with the Pope. But we do not fool the college student who hopes to marry a Catholic girl. He comes to me and tries to tell me that he will not raise his children in the Catholic Church. He is not bitter or angry, only honest and open in his search for faith. He will not force a religion on his children, nor sign promises that he can't in conscience keep. Colleen is with him, watching my eyes as he talks, fearful lest I drive her non-Catholic fiancé from her love. She does not want to leave her Church, but she cannot make her man alter his beliefs. She has been afraid to tell him about the instructions he must take, about the nature of the promises I will ask him to sign. So we talk, hoping to change his honest views and undermine his faith. I approach him gently, calmly, not raising my voice or playing the authoritarian that he has learned to expect in dealing with my Church. But he is stubborn and direct. He wants no double talk, no wily meanderings that only say an uncompromising "No!"

Colleen is listening in fear and Catholic guilt. She attended my classes in school when I told her to marry a Catholic. She has heard since childhood that she is baptized in the one, true Church, and that to abandon her faith is to "go to hell." She senses the futility of our conversation, for she knows the determination of her man and loves him for it. But she watches me, pleading with me to give her love a chance, begging for an exception to our inexorable rules, trying to tell me with an eloquent glance that I am the finality of her hope. She wants to be married at Mass, she wants to grow in the only faith she has ever known, she wants her children to know the comfort of her belief. But this is her man, the man who will father her children and fortify her life, the man who has faith and principles of his own. Can she ignore his rights so as to please her Church? Can she leave him to find a husband who will not compromise the unyielding law of Rome?

Her man talks and listens with dignity. He is a Lutheran, the product of a religious home, independent in his judgment and honest in his dealings with other men. He has friends, a promising future, great hopes for his future children, a warm and abiding love for his future wife. He worked his way through college, served for fourteen months in Vietnam, and has been offered an exciting job. But he is a non-Catholic, not a man, an honest American, a successful student, or a loyal Lutheran. And since he is a non-Catholic, he must follow my dictates or leave!

So he left and Colleen went with him. He could have signed the promises like a thousand others and refused to keep them. He could have taken the instructions and resisted my attempts to snatch away his faith. But he was too honest to pretend, so he left my presence in anger and disgust. I was angry, too, not at Colleen or her courageous young man, but at my arrogant Church and its obsolete law which could attempt to force a man against his conscience in order to marry the woman he loved. It was a coward's law, a despot's law, a law which made a mockery of God.

But I kept the law, and I must keep it still. I must wait for the Pope to change it, or the bishops to seduce the papal court. I must be satisfied with the crumbs that trickle bit by bit from Rome. I can now invite non-Catholics to marry Catholics at Mass, and ask a minister to give a blessing to this union in my Church. I can waive the written promises as long as I get permission and exact these promises with solemn words. I must be satisfied with such meaningless crumbs when I am screaming for a loaf of bread!

Dear God, who will obliterate the arrogance of my Church? Have I not watched a non-Catholic raise his family Catholic, support our Church, and send his children to our schools? Have I not watched his endurance of the religious gibes of his own children, his tolerance of his wife's insistence on rhythm in their bed, his charity to the poor, his honesty in business, his respect in the community? Then have I not seen us refuse to bury him in our Church because he was not a member of our faith? Have I not whispered a pathetic handful of prayers over his body in a mortuary, forbidden to bring his body into my Church, to bless his last remains, even to wear a single vestment of my priesthood? Have I not spoken the few comforting words to the six Catholic children he raised, to the widow and the nineteen grandchildren who loved him and kissed his cold hand until the coffin was sealed, ignoring their pleas for a more decent burial, and explaining my Church's rules to his weeping wife.

She had no answer to my learned theology and canon law. She could only tell me of his love, his gentleness, his kindness to the children. She could only recall the Sundays he shoveled snow to bring the children to Mass. She could only tell me of the times he taught the children their religion, of the days he struggled to support the large family that her Catholic convictions produced, of the nights she turned her back on him to honor a law he did not understand. She knew nothing of history or bigotry or Roman law. She only knew that her husband had died and she wanted to honor her memories of him with the liturgy of her Church. But he was a non-Catholic, an outsider, a non-participator in the privilege of my faith. So we honored him in a funeral parlor with its professional sympathy and its impersonal dismissal of the dead.

Nor could she have Masses said to honor his name. She could offer Masses for a "special intention," but his name could not appear in the lists that were printed in the parish bulletin. I explained all this to her and she thanked me in her tears. I wish she would have turned her back, screamed at me, hated me. But she thanked me, and left me cursing the heartlessness of my Church. I had eaten in this man's home, played golf with him, worried with him about his children, but I could not honor his body with the ritual of my Church. Had I been able to pour a bit of water on his head before he died, to extract a dying wish to be a Catholic, even to hear a nurse say that he had requested a priest, then perhaps I could have buried him from the Church. But he had died a non-Catholic, and I could not reward his family's failure to convert him with a solemn *Requiem*.

The man who is a non-Catholic has known the pride of my Church. The Protestant knows that Catholics are forbidden to worship in his Church lest they be contaminated by heresy. A Catholic can attend a wedding or a funeral in a Protestant Church, but he cannot join in prayer. He comes as a silent spectator, paying his respects to his non-Catholic friend even as he insults his friend's faith. The Catholic can attend a bar mitzvah, if a broad-minded pastor gives his consent. But he cannot pray with the Jews or receive their blessings or share the sacred traditions which antedate his own Church. Jews are especially pitiable because they rejected Christ, especially hard to convert because they take pride in their family.

The man who is a non-Catholic has suffered from the narrowness of the Catholic mind. Catholics do not listen; they have only been taught to defend. They refuse to question what they learned in childhood. They can defend pious superstition with the same ardor with which they embrace key doctrines of their faith. They can uphold a Roman ruling with the fire of a martyr's conviction and ignore it once the bishop pronounces that Saturday, at midnight, it does not apply.

They can criticize non-Catholics as indulgent sinners who dilute the teachings of Christ. They can ridicule ministers and rabbis as unworthy prophets or frauds, laugh at the ceremonies of non-Catholic sects, condemn the vagueness of other moral teachings without recognizing the rigidity of their own. Catholics can attack the non-Catholic's stand on birth control as "selfish compromise" and his position on divorce as "moral chaos." No one escapes our wrath or righteous condemnation. Our papers attack the divorces of Ford and Rockefeller without knowing the circumstances of their private lives. Catholic leaders can question their moral fitness for office, and defend with fervor an alcoholic bishop or a greedy priest. They can scorn welfare programs which attempt to solve a problem without upholding the moral opinions of the Church.

We have alienated our public schools by our criticism of their efforts, by dumping our problem children in their laps, by attacking the teachers who attempted to tell Catholic children there was more than a Catholic view of life. We have attacked professors in our state universities who upheld moral systems different from our own, who described the brutality of the Church in history, who questioned Catholic opposition to the democratic way of life. And in areas of our country where Catholics were in the majority, we have even driven such professors from their posts to shield our students from unpleasant truth. And thus refusing the freedom of speech to others, we have screamed when our own freedoms were put in jeopardy.

We have boycotted movies when our censors were offended, forbade literature which questioned our infallibility or impugned the motives of our Pope, lured advertisers away from magazines which printed articles hostile to us. We could criticize the entire world, mock its standards, ridicule its goals, and not bear the least attack on the policies and programs that we enforced. We made fun of the archaic laws which questioned our bingo and gambling, and were indignant when moderns suggested that our marriage laws were obsolete. It has been our way or no way, and the non-Catholic has suffered from the authoritarian arrogance that characterizes our defense of the Catholic Church.

I am guilty of the wounds that my Church inflicted on the man who is a non-Catholic, because I did not battle or openly protest. And I should have known better as I walked among my fellow men. My optometrist was Jewish, loyal to his relatives and honest in his work. Yet he is a non-Catholic, and I was forbidden to share the bar mitzvah to honor his son lest I give scandal to my calling and my Church. I might give approval to his religion by my presence at his Temple. I might fortify his blindness or delay his conversion to the Catholic Church.

A generous friend was Jewish, married to a Catholic, but married without the permission and blessing of my Church. I was expected to ask him, therefore, to renew his vows in my presence. He was in serious error since he was not married in the Church. His Catholic wife was forbidden the sacraments, and I was expected to insult him by asking him to go through a religious ceremony required by laws that neither he nor I could understand.

Another close friend was a Mason. I used to drink beer with him, to ask his help with programs for the teen-agers, to hear him tell me what Masonry had done to make of him a man. Yet I was expected to convert him, even though I knew he was closer to God than I, more tolerant of sinners, more loyal to his calling.

I toured Europe with religious teachers of every denomination, enjoyed their friendship, laughed and ate with them, marveled at their sincerity, noted the seriousness of their quest. But they were heretics, potential converts, men who knew but half the truth until they joined me in my Church. And

yet how could they so embody the fullness of charity if they
were so severed from the truth? What did they lack if they
worshiped God and loved their fellow man? What could I offer
them in the restricted quality of my own love? Did they need
to know of purgatory, honor Mary, obey the Pope before I
could relax and join with them as friend?

They had more to offer me than I could ever give to them.
They had learned tolerance and lived it in their life. Their
conscience was free and so was their childlike openness to
God. I was the narrow one, the man stuffed with unchanging
dogmas and unyielding codes. I was the intolerant priest, the
fierce judge, the subtle searcher for converts. The man who is
a non-Catholic was the better suited to talk to men of Christ.

And yet I have wounded him and we wound him still. We
invite him to share our friendship when secretly we try to
win him to our side. We enter with him in dialogue, but we
anticipate any motion to come from him. We insult him with
our feigned learning, and lure him with the better public relations which only hide the same narrow theology.

But no longer will I call him "non-Catholic" to reveal that
I divide the world between my kind and his. I will not even
call him "Christian," so varied has this common word become.
Nor will I call him "Jew." I will call him "brother" and hope
he will forgive and understand.

My brother, who does not believe as I, I apologize. I
apologize for the pain I have caused you, for the indignity I
have forced upon your children. I apologize for imposing my
laws upon you, for the arrogance of my public statements, for
the smugness that made me always right. My brother, I denied
you my sacraments and made a mockery of yours. I called my
family loyalty "faith" and called your faith a sham. I laughed
at your ministers, slurred your rabbis and bishops, criticized
your conferences, and undermined your reputation. And for all
this I apologize.

And, my brother, I lied to you when I told you the certainty
of my faith. I live in doubt and shadows as do you. I struggle
to believe amid pain, search to find amid confusion, often

touch a phantom when I try to hold my God. I sound cocky when I recite my doctrines and confident when I resolve the dilemmas of moral law. But I am only a child in search, a weak and frightened one, who struggles with the mystery of faith. I do not believe, I only try to. I do not love, I only make a feeble effort to begin. I am your brother, or want to be, if you will forgive me for the wall I built to separate our hearts.

My brother, I need you, I miss you. I need the loyalty of Israel, the fire of Luther, the discipline of Calvin, the warmth of Wesley, the wisdom of the humanists to speak to me of man. I have lived in suspicion, in tension, in anger, in bitterness, in calumny and righteousness, in narrowness and fear. I have hidden from you my weakness and exaggerated my strength. Now I ask to be your brother, not in simulated love, but in the depths of my own loneliness to join you in the search for the Father Who loves us both alike.

I cannot atone for the injuries of the past. I cannot bring together the many couples whose religious differences tore them apart, the differences I fostered. It only helps to reveal to you how miserable and inhuman I have felt in loyalty to my job. It helps to look forward to the day when my Church will have abandoned its arrogance, when it will not offer its Catholic code to force the conscience of the world. Then there will be no "non-Catholics," there will be only persons, struggling to be honest to themselves. Then I can call you "brother," not Jew or Protestant or non-Catholic, and hope that you will forgive my narrowness and call me "brother," too.

EPILOGUE

One Christmas Eve when I was a little boy, I wandered alone through the darkened streets of my city. It was cold and a softly falling snow was cleaning the sidewalks for an Infant's birth. I was holding my rosary in the pocket of my jacket and whispering the thousand "Hail Marys" that the Irish often say on Christmas Eve. I was at peace with the world and full of joy in the exuberance of my youth. I remember coming home, flushed with the cold, still absorbed in the reverie of that unforgettable night. My mother was playing Christmas carols, my father was reading the paper in his chair. I did not feel like talking, I did not want to disturb the quiet magic of the spell. A couple of my brothers were wrapping packages, one was struggling with a stubborn set of lights. It was a quiet time in a home that seldom stood so still.

I do not know why that night is etched in my memory, I do not know why its music haunts me. Perhaps it is because I knew that night that I belonged to God and that peace is all I want. Perhaps it is because I knew that night that I must be myself. Even now, nothing has changed, the child has grown, and the peace I sought in praying through the snowy streets, I pray and search for still.

I still believe in the power of the priesthood, where sinful

176

men are helped by sinful men. I believe in an authority that stoops to wash a poor man's feet. I believe in a banquet where sinners learn to love, eating in company with their God. I believe in parents who teach their children the beauty that is life. I believe in the words that God has left for men, words that can fashion hope from darkness and turn bitter loneliness into love. And I believe in man, fashioned in mystery by God. I believe in the beauty of his mind, the force of his emotions, the fire and loyalty of his love. I know his weakness, his cowardice, his treachery, his hate. But I believe in him and his thirst for acceptance and love.

Most of all I believe in God and the power of His victory in Christ. I believe in a Resurrection that rescued man from death. I believe in an Easter that opened man to hope. I believe in a joy that no threat of man can take away. I believe in a peace that I know in fleeting moments and seek with boldness born of God. I believe in a life that lingers after this, a life that God has fashioned for His friends.

I believe in understanding, in forgiveness, in mercy, in faith. I believe in innocent children whose eyes are messages from God. I believe in teen-agers, carefree or sullen, whose struggles presage the tempest that is man. I believe in man's love for woman, and hers for him, and in the fervor of this exchange I hear the voice of God. I believe in friendship and its power to turn selfishness to love. I believe in lasting love and the painful growth that it requires. I believe in death and the mystery that it unveils. I believe in eternity and the hope that it affords.

I do not believe in arrogance or pride. I do not believe in the haughtiness of man. I do not believe that laws can crush man's confidence or smother the spirit of God. I do not believe that any ritual can limit divine love or seal the channels that lead a man to God. I do not believe in the unerring judgment of men that ignores the conscience of the simple and sincere.

I am sorry if, in writing this book, I hurt my family, although they are, for the most part, likely to approve. I am sorry to hurt the sisters who taught me from childhood, who asked my blessing as a priest. I am sorry to hurt the priests who forgave me as a child, the priests with whom I labored in the field, the priests whose confidence I shared. I am sorry to hurt the people who listened to my words, who received my absolution, who welcomed me to their homes and offered me their hearts. Their faces swim before me as I write. I am sorry for the pain I may cause, and only the pain I may relieve provides me with the courage and patience to write.

You have heard my story, told as honestly and carefully as I can. You may say that I seek a way of indulgence and compromise, but you are wrong. I do not live without worry or responsible concern. In fact, I have never felt so responsible since I discovered that the Church cannot absorb my conscience, nor replace my mind. Life was easier when I knew where everything fit, when I could lose myself in the structure of a massive organization. There heaven and hell were governed by careful laws. There God's friendship was certain and manageable, and I was satisfied when I kept the Church's rules.

Now I am lost, but free; honest, but afraid; certain, but ever in doubt. I do not fear hell because I cannot fathom it. I do not seek heaven because it offers no image I can grasp. I only struggle to find myself, to love my fellow men, and to hope that in this way I am truly loving God. And in my struggle, I would like the Church to be my servant as Christ promised that it should. I need to know the wonder of the Mass and the comfort of confession amid the perils of my search. But I will not be absorbed, or crowded, or refused permission to be a man. I do not look for the Church to agree with me, for the Church is as various as the feeble men it serves. I only ask that it not refuse to help me because I refuse to be as every other man.

I prize the uniqueness that is mine, and you must do the same. I am God's own child, and no man can tell me that I must live and die as alien. I can respect the Church's goals even as I formulate my own. I can listen to her directives even as I decide how I must live my one and only life. I can pray with brothers who do not agree with me, eat with brothers who find me bold and independent, speak with brothers who regret I ever ceased to be a child. I can do nothing else, for I am a man, designed by God. I need my family, my friends, my Church, but none of these shall forbid me to be myself.

No longer can I stand before my bishop and smile in shy assent when I know he is wrong. No longer will I bow before a pastor when I know his mood has formed the policy of his Church. No longer will I accept in silence the travesties that a dishonest theology has imposed on simple and unsuspecting men. Nor will I leave the Church, even if they demand it of me, for it is my Church.

I shall be a Catholic, a vocal and honest one, even if my superiors forbid me to be a priest. I shall be a Catholic who follows his conscience, demands meaning and relevance from his Church, and will not permit his God to be reduced to empty ritual and all-absorbing law. I shall be a Catholic until one day, perhaps sooner than I think, I shall return to ashes and to God. He will judge me as He must, but I can say to Him as honestly as I say to you: "I have tried to be a man!"

TWENTY FIVE YEARS LATER

When I ended my lecture at Notre Dame University in October of 1967, I had summed up the core of my conflict with the Catholic Church: the compassion and love of Jesus were by time and fear converted to authority, law, and guilt. I had not yet decided to leave the priesthood, but before the end of the talk, I knew I must. I announced my resignation, and tears stored since early childhood flowed unashamedly. It was an honest dialogue, and the audience roared approval for several minutes—approval of what they already felt. The next week a full-page ad appeared in the New York Times from the Notre Dame Alumni Association, saying that reports of enthusiastic approval were untrue. My publisher offered me a half-page ad to reply on October 16, 1967:

"I am resigning from the Catholic priesthood in personal protest against the refusal of the hierarchy of the institutional Church to bring about reform... I can no longer wear the collar nor accept the title of "Father", when the institution I represent can cut off from communion the divorced and remarried, can refuse to admit its error in the matter of birth control, can ignore the plea of priests for marriage, can continue to reduce the principles of Christ to instruments of fear and guilt... I cannot continue to be identified with a power structure that permits only token changes while the screams of millions are not heard...

"My personal protest began almost six years ago. Since then, I have spoken out in every way possible—in the arena of professional theology, before groups of priests, at student gatherings, in magazines and newspapers, on radio and TV, and in a widely circulated book, A

Modern Priest Looks At His Outdated Church. Now I know that the institution and its hierarchy will not listen... I will continue to write, to speak, to fight for the reform of my Church, but I will not be identified with the leadership of a frequently dishonest, frightened, and unchristian institution. I believe that institution is dying and I will begin now to struggle for the rebirth of the Church. I will continue to search for God and meaning, to aid others in that search, to serve God as a free and honest man."

When I wrote those words twenty five years ago, I had no idea how long and painful would be my personal search for God. There was a time when I regretted my Catholic childhood and the years of seminary and priesthood. I felt betrayed and victimized. Now I try to believe that every step along the way is part of God's plan. It does not matter whether I left the priesthood or not, whether I remained a Catholic or followed another path. It only matters that I follow my own inner guide as best I can, and trust that in the process I will find my true identity and personal God. They are the same!

The journey is no different for the primitive in an Amazon rain forest or the pope in Rome. Each of us is a part of the whole, none better or worse, more or less. Our commitment to the light that is given us is our covenant with the universe. Whatever increases our compassion, extends our forgiveness, and ends our judgment of ourselves or others is of God. Some find their way early on in life and never seem to deviate. Others like myself seemed compelled and guided to explore the far reaches of heaven and earth. As once I wrote:

> I left my traditions on the far side of a foggy hill,
> And I will stay away until I can return in sunshine,
> Rescued from them,
> Free to choose which are really mine.

Jesus said that the very hairs of our head are numbered, that every least detail of life has its purpose. There are no "mortal" sins, only mistakes to correct, doubts and fears to resolve, new directions to take that often are very painful. But pain can lead soon or finally to patient suffering, and patient suffering to surrender and resurrection! When I am afraid, I know I am relying solely on my own strength. When I judge or refuse to forgive, I know I am he who remains condemned and unforgiven. It was not my destiny to remain a priest, nor to accept another's truth as mine, but twenty five years have taught me that the Church is only as trapped in fear as I have been.

When I can admit my own wounds and slowly begin to heal, I can look upon the Church without rancor, knowing what it can be, what it must be to come back to the fullness of life. The hierarchy is afraid and cautious when it must be bold. Passion grows stagnant save in scattered pockets. A great, historic structure for hope and healing, creativity and culture lies dormant like a dying shepherd when millions are starving for spiritual pasture and screaming for another way to live. It was Einstein who said that, "Loyalty to petrified opinion never broke a chain or freed a human soul."

The Church must return to the pastoral focus of Jesus. There are hungry to be fed, naked to be clothed, despairing to find hope, aged to be cherished, and hearts of every faith or none to be revered and taught. It was said that Jesus "went about doing good" and the masses flocked to him to escape hoarded human legalities made divine. Such "good" must again be the focus of the Church. Not sin or celibacy, abortion or sex, prosperity or tithing, nor an infallible claim on truth! Not hell and salvation or a patriarchal past denying women's equality! Joy and service must be the focus, not guilt and punishment.

Then the Church with renewed passion and bold leadership, no matter the personal cost, will not board up its buildings, but open up its eyes and heart to the hunger and longing of a world in pain. The "Spirit of God" that in the beginning was midwife to the universe, that once burst into tongues of fire in every language to renew the earth, and that at this instant inhabits every least atom of creation, can raise a dying shepherd to ever greater life. Not through sluggish and token reform, but through the inner wisdom and courage that beckons each of us to a personal and healing transformation. Twenty five years later!

James Kavanaugh

NOTES

PREFACE AND DEDICATION

1. March 12, 1966, Father Stephen Nash (pseudonym), "I Am a Priest—I Want to Marry."

2. Actually, the greatest number of non-Catholic respondents in any given "group" were Mormons, followed by Episcopalians and Baptists.

INTRODUCTION

1. The recent (January, 1967) news of Father Charles Davis, British priest and theologian, Council *peritus*, and spokesman for England's Cardinal Heenan, who left the priesthood and the Catholic Church, is a violent sign of what is taking place within the Catholic Church. My personal opinion is that Father Davis is actually wrong in considering himself disassociated from the Church. He is but one type of "Catholic" who exemplifies the change *within* the Church. A man cannot abandon his tradition and past so easily. Actually, Charles Davis has been produced in the framework of a changing Church, and in a very real sense remains a member of it.

2. Declaration on Religious Freedom, paragraphs 9 and 10.

CHAPTER ONE *The Ideal Becomes the Law*

1. Romans 3:21–28. See S. Lyonet, "De Epistolis Paulinis" pp. 79–87; (Rome: PIB, 1957), Lucien Cerfaux, *The Church in the Theology of St. Paul* (New York: Herder and Herder, 1963), pp. 59 ff. and *passim*.

2. The Catholic scholar begins every argument with a set of presuppositions which make further discussion impossible. See Hans Küng, *The Council, Reform and Reunion* (New York: Sheed and Ward, 1961), pp. 14 ff., wherein he points out that the Church is made up of men and not ideas.

3. The textbooks we used to study theology were the same textbooks that men twice our age had used. There was no room for speculation, only for memorization and conformance.

4. See John McKenzie, *Authority in the Church* (New York: Sheed and Ward, 1966); Marc Oraison, *Love or Constraint?* (New York: Deus Press, 1959), pp. 13 ff.; see also Roger Aubert, *Le probleme de l'acte de foi* (Louvain: Warny, 1958), pp. 677 ff. and *passim*.

5. The discussion on celibacy has grown loud and angry. A good scholarly treatment of the issue is contained in R. J. Bunnik, "The Question of Married Priests," *Cross Currents*, XV (1965), pp. 407–31, and XVI (1965), pp. 81–112. Bunnik, a well-known Dutch theologian, shows the mistaken identification of celibacy with priesthood in the Catholic Church. For an opposing view, see E. Schillebeeckx, "Priesthood and Celibacy," *Documentum Centrum Concilie*, No. 111. Schillebeeckx pursues his theology independently of any empirical evidence, such as Father Fichter's recent study on the problem of clerical celibacy (*National Catholic Reporter*, December, 1966, and January, 1967). See also Leslie Dewart, "The Celibacy Problem," *Commonweal* (April 22, 1966), pp. 146–50, wherein celibacy is seen as a barrier between the priest and the secular man.

For a more ethereal view of celibacy and one revealing the author's unawareness of the realities of priestly existence, see Ida Gorres, *Is Celibacy Outdated?* (Westminster, Md.: Newman, 1965). A more honest view is contained in Pierre Hermand, *The Priest, Celibate or Married*, (Baltimore: Helicon, 1966). Since Hermand is an ex-priest, some Catholic minds can readily dismiss his arguments as mere rationalizations.

6. There is no story more pathetic in its lack of charity than the way the Catholic Church treats its ex-priests.

7. See Yves Congar, *Power and Poverty in the Church* (Baltimore: Helicon, 1964), pp. 111 ff. and *passim*.

8. See J. Ratzinger, "Free Expression and Obedience in the Church," *The Church* (New York: Kennedy, 1963), pp. 194 ff., 212 ff., where he speaks of the "servility of sycophants."

CHAPTER TWO *The Man Who Is a Priest*

1. Will Herberg, *Protestant—Catholic—Jew* (Garden City: Doubleday, 1956); Gerhard Lenski, *The Religious Factor* (Garden City: Doubleday, 1963), pp. 35 ff.; Herve Carrier, *The Sociology of Religious Belonging* (New York: Herder and Herder, 1965), pp. 117 ff.; Edward Wakin and Joseph F. Scheuer, *The De-Romanization of the American Catholic Church* (New York: Macmillan, 1966), pp. 17–54.

2. John Courtney Murray, *The Problem of Religious Freedom* (Westminster, Md.: Newman, 1965), pp. 7–17.

3. See Michael Novak, *A New Generation* (New York: Herder and Herder, 1964), pp. 59 ff.; E. L. Mascall, *The Secularization of Christianity* (New York: Holt, Rinehart and Winston, 1965), pp. 23 ff.

4. See John McKenzie, "Law in the New Testament," a paper delivered to the Canon Law Society of America, October 12, 1965, and to be found in the "Proceedings" of that group.

5. Joseph Fichter, *Religion as an Occupation* (Notre Dame, Ind.: Notre Dame Press, 1961), pp. 220–70.

6. John McKenzie, *Authority in the Church*, pp. 110–22; William DuBay, *The Human Church* (New York: Doubleday, 1966), esp. Chapter 7; Gerhard Lenski, *op. cit.*, pp. 293–304.

7. See Gabriel Marcel, *Creative Fidelity* (New York: Farrar, Straus and Co., 1964), pp. 147–94; Teilhard de Chardin, *The Divine Milieu* (New York: Harper and Row, 1960), pp. 57–66.

CHAPTER THREE *The Man Who Is a Catholic*

1. John McKenzie, *Authority in the Church*, passim; *Theology in the University*, John Coulson, ed. (Baltimore: Helicon, 1964), pp. 25–46.

2. Recently, theological developments have begun to consider the so-called "anonymous Christian," i.e. the sincere searcher of every faith. See Karl Rahner, the great German theologian, in *The Church* (New

York: Kennedy, 1963), pp. 112 ff.; see also Charles Davis, *Theology for Today* (New York: Sheed and Ward, 1962), pp. 65 ff.

3. Daniel Callahan, *The Mind of the Catholic Layman* (New York: Scribner, 1963), pp. 79 ff.

CHAPTER FOUR The Catholic Parish

1. Vatican II simplifies this process: *Decree on Bishops' Pastoral Office in the Church,* paragraph 31 (October 28, 1965).

2. Vatican II offers other norms to determine a pastoral appointment, but such a change in attitude will take a long time to enforce: *Ibid.*

3. Congar-Dupuy, *L'épiscopat et l'église universelle* (Paris: Les Editions du Cerf, 1964), pp. 240 ff.

4. See Canons 451 ff.

5. Bishop Steven Leven, "Priests Without Power," *National Catholic Reporter* (October 27, 1966), p. 10. The *National Catholic Reporter* has, in my mind, been the greatest single publication in America to spark renewal. It has been of special assistance to priests and nuns. The "Sisters' Forum" is an unparalleled effort in journalistic dialogue.

6. *Decree on Bishops' Pastoral Office,* esp. paragraphs 4–10.

7. Gerard Sloyan, "The Parish as Educator," *Commonweal,* special issue (March 25, 1966), p. 20. This entire issue was an outstanding treatment of the problem of parochial renewal. See also Aloysius Church, "Preach the Word," *The Way* (January, 1965), pp. 33–44.

8. *The Word,* ed. by the seminarians of Canisianum, Innsbruck (New York: Kennedy, 1964), pp. 171–248; Charles Davis, *Theology for Today,* pp. 12–24, 44–64; Gregory Baum, "Word and Sacrament in the Church," *Thought* (1963), pp. 199–200; Vatican II, *Dogmatic Constitution on Divine Revelation* (November 18, 1965), esp. Chapter VI.

9. *Martin Luther,* ed. John Dillenberger (Garden City: Doubleday Anchor, 1961), pp. 229–32.

10. Davis, *op. cit.,* pp. 53–55.

11. "DePauw Presents His Case—Rome, Mary, Mass," *National Catholic Reporter* (February 9, 1966), p. 7.

12. See the special issue of *Commonweal*, entitled "Reforming the Parish" (March 25, 1966); Herve Carrier, *The Sociology of Religious Belonging*, pp. 167 ff.

13. Vatican II, *Decree on Bishops' Pastoral Office*, paragraph 30, 2.

14. Charles Davis, *Liturgy and Doctrine* (New York: Sheed and Ward, 1960), pp. 75–92; see the classic letter of Romano Guardini, *Herder Correspondence*, special issue (Spring, 1964), pp. 24 ff.

CHAPTER FIVE *The Loss of Personalism*

1. See John Macquarrie, *Twentieth Century Religious Thought* (New York: Harper and Row, 1963), pp. 193–209, 210–25, 351–70.

2. Jean Moroux, *I Believe* (London: Sheed and Ward, 1955); Romano Guardini, *The Life of Faith* (New York: Deus, 1960), pp. 72 ff.; Joseph Pieper, *Belief and Faith* (New York: Pantheon, 1962), pp. 43 ff.; Richard Butler, O.P., *Themes of Concern* (Garden City: Doubleday, 1966), pp. 15–30.

3. Karl Rahner, *Theological Investigations*, Vol. II (Baltimore: Helicon, 1963), pp. 89–107; also *Moral Problems and Christian Personalism*, Vol. V of Concilium Series (New York: Paulist Press, 1965).

4. J. H. Newman, *Grammar of Assent* (1870) (Garden City: Doubleday Image, 1955), p. 90.

5. See Max Scheler, *On the Eternal in Man* (London: SCM Press, 1960), pp. 281 ff., pp. 297 ff.; Maurice Blondel, *Letter on Apologetics* (New York: Holt, Rinehart and Winston, 1964), *passim*.

6. Ollé-LaPrune, a quote from *La Certitude Morale*, found in Roger Aubert, *Le problème de l'acte de foi*, p. 269.

7. Blondel, *op. cit.*, p. 196.

8. See Emile Poulat, *Histoire, dogma et critique dans la crise moderniste* (Paris: Casterman, 1962); in English, see the Introduction to Blondel's *Letter on Apologetics*, by Trethowan and Dru; also Alec Vidler, *Prophecy and Papacy* (New York: Scribner, 1964); and Gustave Weigel,

"The Historical Background of the Encyclical 'Humani Generis,'" *Theological Studies*, XII (1951), pp. 212 ff.

9. See Cirne-Lima, *Personal Faith* (New York: Herder and Herder, 1965), *passim*; G. Phillips, "Deux tenances dans théologie contemporaire," *Nouvelle Revue Theologique*, 85 (1963), pp. 227 ff.

10. See Karl Rahner, *Theological Investigations*, Vol. II, pp. 235 ff.; Charles Davis, *Theology for Today*, pp. 12 ff.

11. Blondel, *op. cit.*, p. 147.

CHAPTER SIX *The Church of the Legal Code*

1. This is not to deny the efforts of Europe's Karl Rahner, Edward Schillebeeckx, Bernard Haring, or Canada's Gregory Baum, or even America's John Courtney Murray. But even the best of our theologians seem to fear the essential conclusions that should courageously follow their speculation. Rome has made cowards of them all.

2. Karl Rahner's more sophisticated approach to indulgences can be seen in *Theological Investigations*, Vol. II, pp. 175 ff. The people, however, are fed the same involved myths born of medieval superstition.

3. The theologian can admit the honesty of a non-Catholic's faith, but denies him the right to share in the Catholic communion.

4. Newman, *op. cit.*, p. 304.

CHAPTER SEVEN *Confession and Mortal Sin*

1. Hagmaier and Gleason, *Counseling the Catholic* (New York: Sheed and Ward, 1959), pp. 73–93, offers a somewhat balanced view of the problem of masturbation, but "legalism" still leers through the treatment. It is a case of good psychology inhibited by mediocre theology. More balanced approaches are contained in Von Gagern's *The Problem of Onanism* (Westminster, Md.: Newman, 1955), pp. 53–114, and in Marc Oraison, *Love or Constraint?* chapters II–V.

2. Much of the Catholic emphasis on frequent confession is the product of myth and guilt, and not sound theology. See Bernard Leeming, *Principles of Sacramental Theology* (London: Longmans, 1962), pp. 485, 595 ff., and *passim*; Louis Monden, *Sin, Liberty and Law*, pp. 44 ff.

3. See the involved "double-talk" in Ford and Kelly, *Contemporary Moral Theology*, Vol. I, pp. 174–276, wherein man's freedom is taken for granted and obstacles to freedom are considered an exception rather than the normal human condition. Compare this, for example, with Jean Mouroux's *The Meaning of Man* (Garden City: Doubleday Image, 1961), pp. 151–81.

4. See Emmanuel Mounier, *The Character of Man* (New York: Harper, 1956), pp. 268–314; Henri Niel, "The Limits of Responsibility," *Sin* (New York: Macmillan), pp. 33–60; Frederick von Gagern, *Mental and Spiritual Health* (New York: Deus, 1954), pp. 64–76.

5. Piet Schoonenberg, *Man and Sin* (Notre Dame, Ind.: Notre Dame Press, 1965), pp. 25–39; Monden, *op. cit.*, pp. 34–40; Henri Rondet, *The Theology of Sin* (Fides, Notre Dame, Ind.: Fides, 1960), pp. 87 ff. Rondet proposes the right questions, but answers them with legalistic simplicity. For an example of the kind of Catholic scholarship which can find our legalistic view of "mortal sin" in ancient texts, see Hubert Motry, *The Concept of Mortal Sin in Early Christianity*, a dissertation (Washington, D.C.: Catholic University, 1920). Motry can make the Shepherd of Hermas and Justin sound a whole lot like Ford and Kelly.

6. Monden, *op. cit.*, pp. 45 ff. It also should be indicated for the non-professional that the Church omits a detailed or "integral" confession for a serious reason. Thus servicemen entering battle can be given a kind of "group absolution." Scrupulous penitents would also be freed from the obligation of a detailed confession. What better reason could there be for a confession without the listing of sins than an effort to restore relevance and personalism?

7. Hagmaier and Gleason, *op. cit.*, pp. 31–50.

8. Marc Oraison, *Love or Constraint?*, pp. 120–39; Vincent P. Miceli, "Marcel: The Ascent to Being," *Thought* (1964), pp. 395–420; John McKenzie, *Authority in the Church*, pp. 162–74.

9. Schoonenberg, *op. cit.*, pp. 150 ff.

10. *Ibid.*, pp. 98–199; Charles Davis, *Theology for Today*, pp. 139–152; Karl Rahner, *Theological Investigations*, Vol. I, pp. 347 ff.

11. E. A. Speiser, *Commentary on Genesis*, Vol. I of *Anchor Bible* (Garden City: Doubleday, 1965).

12. S. Lyonet, *De Peccato et Redemptione*, Vol. I, *De Notione Peccati*, Chap. VI, "De Epistolis Paulinis," pp. 79–87 (Rome: PIB, 1957); Henri Rondet, *The Theology of Sin*, pp. 29–35.

13. F. X. Durwell, *The Resurrection* (New York: Sheed and Ward, 1961), pp. 202–359; Gabriel Marcel, *Homo Viator* (New York: Harper Torchbook, 1962), pp. 29–67.

CHAPTER EIGHT *The Rules of Courtship*

1. Marc Oraison, "Psychology and the Sense of Sin," *Sin*, pp. 1–32.

2. See Ford and Kelly, *Contemporary Moral Theology*, Vol. I, pp. 141–73.

3. Bishop J. Reuss, *Modern Catholic Sex Instruction* (Baltimore: Helicon, 1964), makes some attempt to recognize the pressure of real-life situations, such as those he calls "situations of dependence." The Bishop, however, believes his title page and ends up giving us the same old ideas with a gentle disposition.

4. Any personal approach to morality is always called by its Catholic opponents "situation ethics." This is a broad term which is supposed to end all discussion. See Ford and Kelly, *op. cit.*, pp. 104–40. Joseph Fletcher's *Situation Ethics* (Philadelphia: Westminster Press, 1966), is a refreshingly new approach to moral problems and it gives a positive place to the individual and the supremacy of love. Fletcher really believes that man is basically good and offers him the chance to become a person. See also the fine chapter "Legal Ethics or Situation Ethics" in Louis Monden's *Sin, Liberty and Law*, *op. cit.*, pp. 73–144. Also Jules Toner, "Focus for Contemporary Ethics," *Thought* (1965), pp. 5–19.

5. Bernard Haring, *The Law of Christ*, Vol. I (Westminster, Md.: Newman, 1963), pp. 35–134.

6. Catholics unquestionably share this "game playing" with others. See the excellent chapter "Sex and Secularization," in Harvy Cox, *The Secular City* (New York: Macmillan, 1965), pp. 192–216, especially pp. 206–208.

CHAPTER NINE *Christian Marriage and Divorce*

1. Rudolph Schnackenburg, *The Moral Teaching of the New Testament* (New York: Herder and Herder, 1965), p. 267.

2. See Enda McDonagh, "Recent English Literature on the Moral Theology of Christian Marriage," in *Moral Problems and Christian*

Personalism, Vol. V of Concilium Series, pp. 130–54; also Bernard Haring, *Marriage in the Modern World* (Westminster, Md.: Newton, 1965), pp. 75–77. Haring supplies the principles which would permit a change in the Church's divorce law, but, typically, hesitates to draw conclusions. John McKenzie, *Authority in the Church*, p. 168, offers an explanation for the Church's fear of change, no matter how urgent the need.

CHAPTER TEN *Birth Control*

1. There have been solid treatises which show the futility of the Church's efforts to base its policy on birth control on the natural law. See Louis Dupre, *Contraception and Catholics* (Baltimore: Helicon, 1964), or Leslie Dewart "Casti Connubii" in *Contraception and Holiness* (New York: Herder and Herder, 1964), pp. 202–310.

2. Actually the *Constitution on the Church in the Modern World* from Vatican II, paragraphs 47–52, reveals that a progress in the Church's thought and in the minds of some theologians has already resolved the birth control problem by casting a giant doubt on the Church's "traditional" stand. See Gregory Baum, "Can the Church Change its Position on Birth Control" in *Contraception and Holiness*, pp. 311–44.

Another important work which shows that the Church will obviously change its present position is the exceptional work of John T. Noonan, Jr., *Contraception* (Cambridge, Mass: Harvard University Press, 1965). Noonan shows the historical effort of the Church to protect certain values in marriage and leaves little doubt as to the necessity of a change in the present birth control "law." Since our understanding of the place of sex in marriage has grown, the marriage "value" reveals that sex has meaning in the lives of married persons even if such sexual expression is "contraceptive." See also Noonan's article "Contraception and the Council," *Commonweal* (March 11, 1966).

An increasing number of priests are giving Catholic women "permission" to use the pill.

3. Perhaps the clearest expression of the Church's traditional stand against birth control is contained in Ford and Kelly, *Contemporary Moral Theology*, Vol. II (Westminster, Md.: Newman, 1963), pp. 235–429. To one who has studied any modern moral theology, the Ford-Kelly position has only historical interest. For a clear exposition of the method of modern theology, see the late Kieran Conley's "Procreation and the Person" in *Contraception and Holiness*, pp. 60–71.

4. See John Marshall, *The Infertile Period* (Baltimore: Helicon, 1963). Dr. Marshall's efforts are sincere and sophisticated. For an incredible attempt to defend the Church's traditional stand and to en-

courage rhythm, see F. J. Ayd, Jr., "The Oral Contraceptives and Their Mode of Action," National Catholic Welfare Conference, pamphlet publication (Washington, D.C.: 1964).

CHAPTER ELEVEN Catholic Schools

1. Andrew Greeley and Peter Rossi, *The Education of Catholic Americans* (Chicago: Aldine, 1966). The Notre Dame study appears to be no more strongly supportive of our educational system than the Greeley-Rossi research.

2. Vatican II's remarks are just as defensive and "unaware" in the school problem as are those of Pius XII's *Encyclical on Christian Education*. See *Declaration on Christian Education*, paragraph 5 ff.

3. Mary Perkins Ryan, *Are Parochial Schools the Answer?* (New York: Holt, Rinehart and Winston, 1964).

4. Herve Carrier, *The Sociology of Religious Belonging*, pp. 138–53.

5. Anthony T. Podovano, *The Estranged God* (New York: Sheed and Ward, 1966), makes an outstanding effort to relate the search of man for God to the best in modern drama and novels.

6. Michael Duclerq, "The Church and the Question of Catholic Schools," *Cross Currents* (Spring, 1965), pp. 200–12; Daniel Callahan, "The Schools," *Commonweal* (January 8, 1965), pp. 473–76.

7. *Shaping the Christian Message*, ed. Gerard S. Sloyan (New York: Deus, 1963).

8. *Theology and the University*, ed. John Coulson (Baltimore: Helicon, 1964), pp. 107–88.

9. Vatican II seems to offer some approval of this; see *Decree on Christian Education*, paragraph 9.

10. The Church's neglect of the Newman apostolate on the state university campus has filled volumes of periodical literature in the last few years. Newman Club chaplains are among the most talented and hardworking of the priests in the Church. Their apostolate is surely among the most neglected.

CHAPTER TWELVE Life in the Convent

1. See Canons 520–27.

2. Vatican II asks for generous adaptations: Decree on the Appropriate Renewal of Religious Life, paragraph 3.

3. Arturo Paoli, "Obedience," Cross Currents (Spring, 1965), pp. 275–94.

4. Sister Maureen O'Keefe, Christian Love in Religious Life (New York: Regnery, 1966), wherein a sister is encouraged to enjoy the human experiences which are a part of any mature life. It is hard to believe that such a book would have to be written, but it actually does.

5. See interview with Margaret Mead, "Sisters in Modern Society," National Catholic Reporter (March 30, 1966), p. 11. The religious need many such interviews before they decide on the value of their "witness."

6. The problem of the renewal of religious life, so vital to aggiornamento, was treated with platitudes by Vatican II, and most orders are giving the Council the response which it deserves. The sisters are generally as defensive about their "irrelevance" as was Vatican II, and they continue to trouble themselves with much concern about trivial changes.

7. Christopher F. Mooney, Teilhard de Chardin and the Mystery of Christ (New York: Harper and Row, 1966). Christ assumes meaning in the world of men in Chardin's view. He must be found in a Christian's love for others and not in a self-centered form of hypnosis amid personal frustrations. The "life of Christ" spirituality which has filtered through the sisters' meditation books is simply bad theology. We have no biography of Christ, only one of Christ in His Church.

8. Sister Charles Borromeo, "Poverty and Property in Religious Life," National Catholic Reporter (June 1, 1966).

THE AUTHOR

James Kavanaugh exploded onto the American scene in 1967 with his national best-seller, *A Modern Priest Looks At His Outdated Church*. The New York Times called it: "A personal cry that goes to the heart of the troubles plaguing the Roman Catholic Church." A year after *Modern Priest*, he publicly left the priesthood in a dramatic lecture at Notre Dame University. A year later, he wrote another best-seller, *The Birth Of God*, which explored the historic origins of such myths as hell, original sin, celibacy, sexual codes, and infallibility etc.

In the early 70's, living in poverty in a decrepit New York residence hotel, he wrote his first poetry book, *There Are Men Too Gentle To Live Among Wolves*. Ignored by New York publishers, it was finally printed by a small company in Los Angeles. To date it has sold over a million copies. Its impact is Kavanaugh's poetic gift and honest insight into what men and women can be when they refuse to be controlled by guilt, fear, and the respectable addiction of "success".

A dozen poetry books have followed *Men Too Gentle*, as well as powerful novels, and books of non-fiction, each written from the depths of his own heart and experience. The rebel priest became the people's poet, frequently likened to Mark Twain and Will Rogers. He has been lauded by Carl Rogers, Carleton Whitehead, William Conrad, Patrick J Hughes, Dear Abby, Wayne Dyer, and others.

James Kavanaugh possesses a charisma exciting audiences and filling lecture halls with passion and eloquence, humor and tenderness, bold insights and unadorned truth. It was San Francisco's favorite Irish bartender who summed up his power: "With a bar stool, a decent mike, his poetry, and five minutes, Kavanaugh can reduce a Friday night bar crowd to attentive silence, quiet tears, and the most outrageous laughter."

He has read his poetry worldwide in Manila, Bangkok, Munich, Toronto and others. He received a wild, standing ovation in China. He continues to write, travel, "find his freedom in the center of his soul".

Information About Books, Tapes And Appearances
By James Kavanaugh

In September 1990, all rights to James Kavanaugh books were purchased by Steven J Nash who is now the exclusive publisher of Kavanaugh's books and tapes. For information, write:

STEVEN J. NASH PUBLISHING
P. O. Box 2115 Highland Park, IL 60035
or call: 1-708-433-6731

BOOKS BY JAMES KAVANAUGH

A Modern Priest Looks At His Outdated Church: The 1967 best-seller reprinted in it's entirety with a new introduction. Dr. Carl Rogers said, " It is one of the most moving human documents I have ever read! In an earlier day the author would have been burned at the stake... " Psychology Today said " This book will change the world! "

There Are Men Too Gentle To Live Among Wolves. The James Kavanaugh classic in its 67th printing! He writes: "I am one of the searchers... We searchers are ambitious only for life itself, for everything it can provide... we want to love and be loved, to live in a relationship that will not...prevent our search, not lock us in prison walls..."

Will You Be My Friend? *(57th printing)* Kavanaugh writes: "Friendship is freedom, is flowing, is rare... It trusts, understands, grows, explores, it smiles and weeps. It does not exhaust or cling, expect or demand. It is— and that is enough—and it dreams a lot!"

Laughing Down Lonely Canyons. Kavanaugh confronts human loneliness and fear. He writes: "This is a book for the barely brave like me who refuse to abandon their dream... It is for those who want to make of life the joy it was meant to be, who refuse to give up no matter the pain..."

From Loneliness To Love. Kavanaugh writes: "To move from loneliness to love means to take a risk, to create the kind of personal environment and support we need. This is a book of hope and reassurance that love is available and loneliness can end."

Search: A Guide For Those Who Dare Ask Of Life Everything Good And Beautiful. *(Prose)* "**Search** provides 12 proven principles to move from self doubt through self awareness to self love. It is a celebration of one's creativity and unique beauty, rising from practical psychology to the spiritual power of our Inner Being in a journey to wholeness."

Today I Wondered About Love. *(formerly, Faces In The City)*. This book was written in San Francisco and captured the soul of that most human of cities. Herein are some of Kavanaugh's most profound and gently humorous reflections on the man-woman experience and the quest for personal freedom.

Maybe If I Loved You More. These passionate, lyrical poems confront forces that numb our senses and corrupt our values. Kavanaugh challenges us to be fully human, to move past private fears to simplicity and joy: "So much of life is spent trying to prove something...Maybe if I loved you more, I wouldn't have to prove anything!"

Sunshine Days And Foggy Nights. This work contains Kavanaugh's most tender love poems, like the wondrous *Fragile Woman*: "too tender for sex, who will surely die—if tonight I do not love you." He speaks of the energy of any creative life: "The work I find most significant drains the least energy...my distractions are usually more creative than my resolutions."

Winter Has Lasted Too Long. Kavanaugh sings of personal freedom and real love in a superb preface: "We shall be as free as we want, as mad as we are, as honest as we can. We shall accept no price for our integrity...This book is a heart's recognition that truth matters, love is attainable, and spring will begin tomorrow."

Walk Easy On The Earth. A book inspired by Kavanaugh's years spent in a remote cabin in the California gold country. "I do not focus on the world's despair, I am forever renewed by spring splashing over granite rocks, or a cautious deer emerging into twilight. I know then that I will survive all my personal fears and realize my finest dreams."

A Village Called Harmony-A Fable. A powerful, eloquent prose tale that touches the deepest chords in the human struggle of lust and love, passion and peace. Dear Abby says: "It is a powerful tale of our times. A classic! I loved it!'

Celebrate The Sun: A Love Story. A moving prose allegory about the life of Harry Langendorf Pelican, dedicated to "those who take time to celebrate the sun—and are grateful!" A stirring tale that touches the very core of loving oneself.

The Crooked Angel. James Kavanaugh's only children's story tells of two angels "with crooked little wings" who escape from isolation and sadness through friendship and laughter... A particular Christmas delight. Says Goldie Hawn: "My children loved it! So did I."

Tears And Laughter Of A Man's Soul. James Kavanaugh writes: "Men are not easy to know, even by other men...It's a rare woman who understands men...we hope another marriage, a secret affair, or more income will revive us...ingrained habits only assume a new addictive form, depression fills a vacuum of dead dreams...the path to freedom and joy is more exciting than difficult."

Quiet Water: The Inspirational Poems Of James Kavanaugh. In this powerful new edition of his own favorites, Kavanaugh gives hope and courage when life's most difficult passages seem impossible to endure. He writes with the wisdom and compassion born of his own painful discovery of the path to peace and joy. A perfect gift for a struggling friend!..."There is quiet water in the center of your soul..."

Mystic Fire: The Love Poems Of James Kavanaugh. All the passion, romance, and tenderness, as well as the humor and pain of love unfold in this beautiful new edition of Kavanaugh's favorite love poems. Men and women of any age, will find herein the perfect gift, on any occasion, celebrating the expression of love... "Love grew like some mystic fire around my heart..."

In addition to his books Kavanaugh also has a selection of poetry readings and lectures on audio tape available through Steven J. Nash Publishing.

The Creative Process--Creativity reflects one's uniqueness, rather than imitating what is culturally acceptable. The creator is by definition a rebel.

In Search Of One's Self--Identity and self esteem begin and end with honesty, and the acceptance of who I am now. Denial prevents change and growth.

Man and Woman: A Time For Healing--It is time for blaming to end, for awareness and real communication to begin. Kavanaugh's humor softens a tough subject.

There Are Men Too Gentle--Kavanaugh performs his poetry to an original score by Elmer Bernstein and a full orchestra.

Poetry Of James Kavanaugh--William Conrad does a spectacular reading of Kavanaugh poetry with original music by Shelly Mann.

Of Love, Life, And Laughter--A four tape collection of love poems read by James Kavanaugh, with original music by Leigh Bowser.

Search: A Guide For Those Who Dare--A two tape commentary by James Kavanaugh, covering the twelve principles of his best-selling book, **Search: A Guide For Those Who Dare.**